MW01223031

THE ALMIGHTY

God's Holy Attributes & Their Meaning For Your Life

A 30-Day Meditation

Printed by Kindle Direct Publishing,
An Amazon.com Company

ISBN: 978-1-0824288-3-8

The Scripture versions cited in this book are identified in appendix "English Versions," which hereby becomes a part of this copyright page.

Cover & interior design: Eric Dean
Cover photo: Shutterstock®

THE ALMIGHTY

God's Holy Attributes & Their Meaning For Your Life

A 30-Day Meditation

BRENT SABA

"Who is God? Most answers to this question from theologians focus on the divine attributes, the character and characteristics of the Deity. Devotional literature, especially that which is written for daily use, tends to focus on practical application, without much attention to the doctrinal foundation. In this thirty-day devotional, Saba encourages Christians to refocus our lives on the attributes of the God we worship and serve. Each daily reading unpacks an attribute from the Scriptures and then encourages the reader to live out these key doctrines. This is a theologically rich treatment of the character of God yet written in a non-technical and accessible style. When read carefully and applied conscientiously, the reader will be increasingly transformed in godliness."

THIS IS A THEOLOGICALLY RICH TREATMENT OF THE CHARACTER OF GOD YET WRITTEN IN A NON-TECHNICAL AND ACCESSIBLE STYLE.

Glenn R. Kreider, Ph.D.
Professor of Theological Studies, Dallas Theological Seminary

"Believers want God to be all-loving; but he is so much more than that! Brent has shown from the Scriptures a balance of the character qualities of The Almighty! And each day also offers a challenge as to how believers can apply this truth. Practical. Simple. Doable. I encourage your taking the 30-day journey."

PRACTICAL. SIMPLE. DOABLE.

Ed Lewis
President of CE National, a Church Effectiveness ministry

"On the glorious splendor of your majesty,
and on your wondrous works,
I will meditate."

PSALM 145:5 (ESV)

Dedication

To the church, the Bride of Jesus Christ, for whom He gave His life to make holy. I dedicate this book to you and hope its message helps build, equip, and refresh you in the faith.

Acknowledgements

In many respects this devotional is a culmination of nearly twenty years following Jesus Christ. While the concept of this book — a meditation on God's character and nature which leads to life application — has been in the making for a while, the insights have come from many years of discovering what it means to know and love God. Along the way there have been individuals who have poured into me and helped shape who I am today, and to them I am eternally grateful.

First and foremost, Almighty God. Without your love poured out on the cross and the victory won over death, I would not be who I am or have the hope of eternal life. To my Creator and Sustainer, Savior and Lord, may the concepts in this book bring great honor to Your Name.

To my parents — without your love and support growing up I would not have had the opportunities I have had in life or be where I am. From the bottom of my heart, thank you.

Those who encouraged me in my early walk with God — Charles Bloomfield, who first explained the gospel to me; James VanDuzer, who was my first Bible teacher; and David Scott, who provided rich insights into the faith — your godly example was truly formative.

My home church pastor growing up, Larry Humberd, who provided me with opportunities to speak about the gospel and helped disciple me in the faith — you are a true example of a shepherd and a constant encouragement to many.

My Bible professors at Grace College — Dr. David Plaster, Dr. Mark Soto, Dr. Brent Sandy, and Dr. Skip Forbes — from you I gained a deeper appreciation for the Word of God and a renewed hunger to learn. I still read the late Dr. Plaster's systematic theology syllabus today…coffee stains and all!

Those who supported me with opportunities to lead and serve during my time at Grace College — Ed Lewis, TK Kurtaneck, and Dr. James H. Joiner — I learned so much from each of you and look back at those early years with great joy.

My Bible Exposition, Theological Studies, Pastoral Ministries, World Missions, and Greek and Hebrew professors at Dallas Theological Seminary — Dr. Mark M. Yarbrough, Dr. Steven J. Bramer, Dr. Ronald B. Allen, Dr. Michael J. Svigel, Dr. Nathan D. Holsteen, Dr. J. Lanier Burns, Dr. John D. Hannah, Dr. Larry J. Waters, Dr. Linden D. McLaughlin, Dr. Glenn R. Kreider, Dr. Victor D. Anderson, Dr. Charles W. Dickens, Dr. Timothy S. Warren, Dr. Paul E. Pettit, Dr. Barry D. Jones, Dr. Gordon H. Johnson, Dr. George M. Hillman, Dr. Michael Pocock, Dr. Joseph D. Fantin, Dr. Buist M. Fanning, Dr. Terri Moore, Dr. Robert B. Chisholm, and Dr. Dorian G. Coover-Cox — the training I received during my four year Master of Theology program was truly invaluable. Your service to the Kingdom in equipping men and woman to *teach truth* and *love well* has left an imprint worldwide, and on my life.

And finally, to those who directly impacted the creation of this book: Christina Delgado, who worked diligently for six months to edit and re-edit each chapter; Dr. Steven D. Anderson, who encouraged the concept and publication of this book; Lance Reiss, who continued to lift up this book in prayer; and Jonathan Hallett and Matthew Baldwin who took time to read early versions of my manuscript — thank you for your affirmation and friendship.

Contents

PREFACE

THE GREATNESS OF GOD

THE GOODNESS OF GOD

EPILOGUE

APPENDIX

A 30-Day Meditation

It is not by accident you are holding this book. Before time began God knew about your life, this exact moment in time, and the 30-day meditation you are about to encounter through these pages. It is my prayer that as you take time to read and reflect on each chapter, you would be in awe of the incomparable greatness and goodness of God. I pray that the deeper and richer insights into God's likeness and character which you gain through this reading would transform the way you view God, yourself, and the world around you. The Bible says, "*...let God transform you into a new person by changing the way you think.*"[1]

For most, the 21st Century world has conditioned the mind to think, process, and "produce results" quickly — to our own spiritual detriment. While one can place their faith in Christ and be indwelt by the Holy Spirit in an instant, the development of the inner spiritual relationship with God does not work in this manner. The journey of knowing and loving God is a one of a lifetime. The church must learn to draw near to God and think upon Him regularly; letting our love for God and others flow out of our knowledge of Him. The Bible says, "*And this is my prayer: that your love may abound more and more in knowledge and depth of insight.*"[2]

A.W. Tozer once said, "Were we able to extract from any man a complete answer to the question, 'What comes into your mind when you think about God?' we might predict with certainty the spiritual future of that man."[3] Indeed, the answer to this question is the most important thing about you, directing the entire course of your life.

Because we were made in the image of God, our thoughts and words have power to alter reality — whether positively or negatively — for good or for evil. This is true both in how we view our self and how we interpret the world around us. It is equally true in how we view God.

During your 30-day meditation, you will discover that our most significant thoughts are our thoughts about God and our most powerful words are our words for God. Mighty thoughts and powerful words for God lead to pure, elevated spiritual living; whereas diluted thoughts and muddled words for God lead to powerless living.

While this is true for the individual, it is equally true for the church. Our messages and prayers tend to center around a man-focused paradigm where God largely exists to bless us and help us. Seldom does the church center its activity around the knowledge of God's character and nature in a manner that transforms our faith.

Modern day Christians know little of the contemplative life, one that centers itself around the essence of who God is. Somewhere along the way the church lost perspective of its sheer reverence and adoration of God. While we hear and sing descriptions for God like "holy," "righteous," and "omnipotent," the reality is that for most these words have little meaning.

If the church is to be relevant in the 21st Century in our worship, discipleship, teaching, and evangelism, we must faithfully pass down to the next generation a pure faith — a faith that once more elevates our thoughts and words for God and transforms us from the inside out. A faith that stands in awe of the brilliance of One whom oceans of ink could not be written.

My Daily Devotion

THE GREATNESS & GOODNESS OF GOD

Each daily devotional reading is organized in the same sequential order:

First, we will ***define*** the attribute of God and how it describes His character and nature.

Second, we will ***discover*** how the attribute interconnects with the Person and Work of Jesus Christ — the Great Mediator between God and man.

Third, we will seek to ***deduce*** principles for the Christian life through interacting with God's attribute and the gospel. A proper understanding of who God is and what Jesus has done should transform our lives from the inside out.

Taking It Further: Each daily reading will conclude with a ***Main Idea***, a ***Verse to Memorize***, and a ***Question to Consider***; helping facilitate further meditation.

EPILOGUE

A supplementary chapter, "***Meditating on God's Holy Attributes***" is included to help provide further application towards cultivating a lifelong pursuit of meditating on God.

APPENDIX

For additional resources, over 100 theological Definitions and Concepts, 250-plus References, and twenty-two English Versions of the Bible is included.

"Instead, let the Spirit renew your thoughts and attitudes. Put on your new nature, created to be like God — truly righteous and holy."

EPHESIANS 4:23-24 (ESV)

Preface

THINKING RIGHTLY OF GOD & HIS HOLY ATTRIBUTES

For who is God, besides the LORD?
2 SAMUEL 22:32A (NASB)

And instead of worshiping the glorious, ever-living God, they worshiped idols made to look like mere people...
ROMANS 1:23 (NLT)

AN ATTRIBUTE IS *WHAT GOD HAS REVEALED AS TRUE OF Himself* — the qualities of God that constitute who He is in His basic character and nature.

In attempts to understand God better, we will classify His attributes in two primary categories: Greatness and Goodness.[1]

The Greatness of God

The Greatness of God, or what may be described as the incommunicable attributes, *are those qualities which belong to God and none other*, such as His all-powerful, all-present, eternal, unchanging nature. God's incommunicable attributes are what differentiates His divinity verses His shared attributes with man. Because God is divine, His authority pervades in every attribute, for all that God is and does is supremely perfect. To use an example, God's love is infinite and unvarying while man's love is imperfect and subject to change.

The Goodness of God

The Goodness of God, or what may be described as communicable attributes, are the moral qualities of God which man can also have and demonstrate in relationship — such as goodness, kindness, grace, mercy, love, faithfulness, justice, joy and peace. Because man was made in the image of God, we were created to reflect God's moral attributes perfectly. Because of the Fall, man falls short of living up to God's moral standard and are in need His forgiveness and grace. Morality for the sake of being good was never the goal, for even our good works are tainted by our sinful nature, rooted in selfish desire. Rather, true morality is loving God and others with a pure heart.

God's attributes are sometimes seen as conflicting with one another, such as His wrath and love. When these attributes are understood properly, however, this is not the case.

Distinction Between God's Character and Nature from Divine Roles and Acts

In contrast to positive statements that affirm what the attributes of God are, explaining what the attributes of God are not helps to clarify the distinction between God's character and nature from His divine Roles and Acts.

For example:

God's attributes should not be confused with *His Roles,* such as Creator or Preserver, or *His Acts,* such as creating, guiding, and preserving. These roles and acts should be understood as flowing from the divine attributes of God's Supremacy and Sovereignty respectively.

God's attributes also should not be confused with the special roles of the Holy Trinity — The Father, The Son, and The Holy Spirit. While the special roles of each Person are unique, the Holy Trinity cooperates harmoniously in this work and are one in divinity.

Additionally, God's attributes should not be understood as part of who He is or how He may express Himself at one time or another. Rather, God's attributes should be understood as *who God is every moment in every situation.* God cannot be one attribute and not the rest of His attributes at the same time. We will explore the concept of God's unitary nature further in this book.

Finally, God's attributes should not be perceived as the mental conception we project upon Him, for the finite mind can never grasp the infinite, nor does our experience or opinion determine who God is.

Maintaining Balanced Thinking

We are prone to gravitate towards one or two attributes we especially like or help us in time of need while dismissing the attributes we do not like or deem to be less beneficial. Because this is so, we must relearn to see the beauty of each attribute and realize that God is every attribute in every circumstance. No attribute is true without all others being simultaneously true.

God's attributes are embodied together in perfect harmony, but also in a balanced tension. God is love and mercy, but God is also just and detests sin. God is gracious and forgiving, but God is also of judgment and wrath. God is Holy. We must be careful, therefore, to not promote one attribute while demoting another but to reverently think rightly of God in proper worship.

The Fall and Humanity's Posture of Worship

In the beginning, when God created the heavens and the earth, day and night, land and sea, and all that fills them, He pronounced the works of His Hands as simply *"good."* Yet when God made Adam and Eve, He created them in His image and His likeness, pronouncing His final work as *"very good,"* for they were God's masterpiece. Adam and Eve were given godlike responsibility over the Garden of Eden to tend to it and to rule over it. Yet, God set boundaries for their protection, setting before them life or death. They were free to eat of every tree, but they were forbidden to eat of the tree of the knowledge of good and evil lest they perish.

When the serpent tempted Adam and Eve to eat of the forbidden fruit, he knew their disobedience would alter their relationship with God and their perception of Him, *"The serpent said to the woman, "You surely will not die! For God knows that in the day you eat from it your eyes will be opened, and you will be like God, knowing good and evil."*[2]

By deliberately disobeying God, Adam and Eve exchanged the truth of God for a lie and committed themselves to that lie. By believing the lie that they could be their own god and revolt against God's authority, their view of God and posture before Him dramatically shifted. Instead of remaining in a posture of worship before God as King, their actions fueled by their doubt and challenging God's authority cost them an eternal price — spiritual and physical death. No longer would Adam and Eve be blessed with the abundance of perfect life in the Garden but would be forced to live an arduous life full of labor, opposition, and death.

Sin, in its basic nature, usurps God's rightful place in your life by attempting to dethrone God and enthrone self, proudly declaring, "I am god!" The Bible says that seeking to be like God in His deity was the fall of Satan[3] and, subsequently, the fall of humanity since the first man and woman were created. Consequently, humanity has a natural tendency toward viewing God and self incorrectly and are prone to fashion a god after a mental concept that is suitable to oneself. The Bible says, "*Instead of honoring the divine greatness of God, who lives forever, they traded it for the worship of idols — things made to look like humans...*"[4]

The Consequence of the Fall

Because of the fall, sin has spoiled every one of our faculties including the mind, the will, the emotions, and even the conscience. Consequently, our perception of God is woefully altered. Instead of properly bearing and reflecting the image of God to the world — our God-given mandate — our faculties deceptively invert our ability to know and reflect God properly. Sin misleadingly makes one believe of God as less than He is and oneself as greater than they are. In other words, instead of holding high views of God and low views of man, we hold low views of God and high views of man. Because of sin, we are all predisposed toward wanting authority and challenging God's place in our life.

In describing Satan, the Bible says, "*He has always hated the truth, because there is no truth in him. When he lies, it is consistent with his character; for he is a liar and the father of lies.*"[5] Satan is not only the father of all blatant lies, but he is also the master of all deception. Like the serpent's crafty use of questioning in the Garden, Satan also uses his craft to pose his schemes as good whispered to our hearts. The Bible says, "*...for Satan himself masquerades as an angel of light.*"[6] We must be very wise and discerning in how we approach the subject of understanding God. If we are honest, most of us are convinced we see God as He really is. We do not intentionally try to distort our perceptions of Him. This is where "unintentional" wrong views of God may seem innocent enough, but it is actually deception of the mind and heart — a monstrous, idolatrous sin that substitutes the true God for a false one.

The Need to Realign Our Thoughts Toward God

One may ask, then, what are concrete examples that I may see this concept more clearly in my life? The time will come. For now, the goal is to be aware and acknowledge that as fallen people we truly need God more than we realize — including viewing Him rightly.

As we contemplate the attributes of God, we seek to properly understand and realign our thoughts of Him so that we may reflect His character as His image bearer to the world. While God is in many ways incomprehensible, there are answers about His character and nature that are both full and satisfying. Answers that reverent reasoning and the humble heart may lay hold of.

THE GREATNESS OF GOD

DAY 1

THE SELF-EXISTENCE OF GOD

Before the mountains were born or you brought forth the whole world, from everlasting to everlasting you are God.
PSALM 90:2 (NIV)

...the King of kings, and Lord of lords, who alone has immortality, who dwells in unapproachable light.
1 TIMOTHY 6:15B-16A (ESV)

God simply is.

In the beginning, before the origin of space, time, and matter, God always was. Heaven did not exist, where His presence is now distinctly manifested, or earth to receive His attention. [1] God was alone and perfectly complete in His Being. He was not obligated to create, nor was there any need when He said, *"Let there be light,"* [2] or *"Let us make man in our image."* [3] God simply chose to create out of His sovereign will and for His own good pleasure.

Origin is a word that applies to created things. Anything created is not God. Origin separates that-which-is-God from that-which-is-not-God. All things had a cause, but God is uncaused. A child who asks, "Where did God come from?" must be told that God had no beginning, God simply *is*. The child will find this concept to be altogether strange and perplexing since it introduces an entirely new, unfamiliar paradigm. It is difficult to comprehend something always existing because it defies the way our world operates and the construct of our mind.

It is a humbling thought to consider a Being who is outside the sphere of our mental comprehension. One who is self-existent, self-sufficient, infinite, eternal, accountable to none and needs none. When we try and think steadily upon such a Being the human mind collapses with exhaustion upon the consideration of One who dwells outside of time and space and simply is. The Bible says, *"How great is God — beyond our understanding!"*[4]

The wise philosopher of ages past and the educated scientist of today ask the same questions, but they come up empty to One who will not submit to their level of reasoning or curious inquiries. Indeed, God cannot be found through philosophical reason, nor can He be found through scientific methods. He can only be found by the heart.

Self-Centered Reality

Because of the fall, we are all prone toward creating a self-centered reality rather than a God-centered reality. The natural mind holds low views of God and high views of self. Stated differently, we reduce, diminish, or adjust God in our mind to make Him fit what is acceptable to us. In doing so, God becomes sidelined and only applicable when we need Him. Instead of God at the center, we place ourselves — our world, our wants, and our needs — at the center.

For many in our day and age, God has been reduced from the God of the universe to the god of spirituality. While many believe in and are interested in God, their views of Him remain inadvertently self-centered. To many, God is pluralistic — a blend of all religions — and desires to bring utopia into our life and the world. The god of spirituality does not judge sin but works for the good of all toward a greater utopic end. On the surface, the god of spirituality appears to have well-meaning intentions, but at the root, its form centers around the creation of a god that is suitable to oneself. Whatever attributes of God one finds acceptable are kept while the attributes of God one finds unacceptable are reduced or left out entirely.

As an analogy, let's use a vase with larger stones and small pebbles. The vase represents our mind and heart, the larger stones represent what is most important to us while the smaller stones are of lesser priority. The larger stones will be God and smaller be self, or the opposite, self being the larger stones leaving God the smaller stones. The sinful nature is naturally bent toward filling the mind and heart with a self (large rocks) and then filling in smaller spaces with God (small pebbles). As result, we place self on the Throne of our lives, meanwhile reducing and adjusting God to fit around us.

Christ's Reversal of Self-Centeredness

To save us completely from our fallen state, Christ must rectify the predisposition in our nature toward selfhood in order to create in us a new desire to place God at the center. He must recalibrate our view of Him and the world around us so that we hold esteemed views of God and humble views of self. He must create in us a new mind and heart — one that no longer lives for self but for God alone. The Bible says, *"And*

He died for all so that those who live should no longer live for themselves, but for the One who died for them and was raised."[5]

Taking It Home

What impression, therefore, should these truths impress upon our life?

First, since we were created by the eternal, uncreated God, we must ask God to help us hold high views of Him. He alone is worthy of all worship.

Second, knowledge of God's self-existence ought to transform the way we view ourselves. Realization that we are created and utterly dependent upon other created things such as food, water, and oxygen should humble the pretentious heart. Without God we are nothing and can do nothing. We must ask God to help us hold a humble view of self and to treasure Him above our next breath.

Third, since God is self-existent, our need for him reaches deeper than our daily physical needs. Sin has cleverly ingrained in each one of us the lie that selfhood is good. We perceive money, material possessions, achievements, level of education, intelligence, status, position, and authority as valid testaments of our independence. However, the truth is any one of these can be wiped out in an instant. We often place more faith upon our capabilities — although they came from God — than we do in God Himself.

Let us learn the lesson from King Nebuchadnezzar who built up a powerful kingdom. Instead of acknowledging God, he was loaded with self-pride for the work of his hands. Because of his arrogance, God wiped Nebuchadnezzar clean...and it wasn't until he repented of his arrogance and acknowledged the Living God that Nebuchadnezzar's kingdom was restored.[6]

Lastly, since the Eternal God created all that is seen from that which is unseen, the daily realities of our existence ultimately point back to God. Because all things come from and are derived from God, so too, all aspects of our reality find their answer in Him. This does not mean that we will always *receive* the answer to our questions, but it does mean that we can *trust* the Self-Existent One who created us. It makes sense, then, to get to know our Creator better.

DAY 1

The Self-Existence of God

MAIN IDEA: Without God I am nothing.

VERSE TO REMEMBER: *"Before the mountains were born, or you brought forth the whole world, from everlasting to everlasting you are God."* Psalm 90:2 (NIV)

QUESTION TO CONSIDER: What areas of my life do I place more trust than in my Creator?

O God, You alone are self-existent;
From nothing, You created all things,
You spoke and life came to be;
Who is like You, O Eternally Uncreated?
From Your Hand am I satisfied.

DAY 2

THE SELF-SUFFICIENCY OF GOD

The Father has life in himself, and He has granted that same life-giving power to His Son.
JOHN 5:26 (NLT)

He existed before anything else, and He holds all creation together.
COLOSSIANS 1:17 (NLT)

GOD ALONE IS SELF-SUFFICIENT.

Just as God had no beginning, dwells outside of time and space, and simply *is*, God is also wholly sufficient within Himself. The very designation given by God to Moses, "*I AM*"[1] presupposes the eternal, independent nature of His Being. The Name suggests that God is not an object of limitation or measurement; on the contrary, it affirms that God is always present, always free to be and to act as He wills. God is not dependent upon anything or anyone. If there were even a speck in existence that God were dependent on in any way, shape, or form, that other would be god. Simply put, God is the One who contains all and gives all that can be given. He can receive nothing that He has not first given. God exists for Himself, but human beings exist for the glory of God.

If God were to have a need, He would have an incomplete nature. Need is a word that describes a dependency on that-which-is-created and cannot be applied in describing the Creator. We may never know every reason why God chose to create, but we can know that He did not create for some unfulfilled need within Himself.

On the contrary, every created thing needs God for every conceivable aspect of its existence. There is not one molecule of your being that is not dependent on and held together by God. The Bible says, *"He existed before anything else, and he holds all creation together."* [2]

Unbelief and Self-Sufficiency

God is supreme in His Being. Nothing can be raised up above Him, and nothing is beyond Him. Even if human beings choose not to believe in God or His self-sufficient, supreme nature, God is still God. Unbelief is the deadly opiate of the mind and creates a strong sense of independence from God. This perversion of faith places trust in one's own sufficiency rather than God. Self-sufficiency creates the illusion that God is unnecessary or at best periphery to one's life. God alone trusts in Himself; all others must trust in Him. Unbelief and self-sufficiency are the residual decay from the fall and ultimately destroys the soul.

Turning from Pride of Self

God cannot be discovered through mere reason. God is a Personal God, not a philosophical or religious construct.

The Bible says that *"God is Spirit"* [3] which means He can only be known spiritually. When Nicodemus came to Jesus in earnest, he discovered that the way to God is to be born again of the Spirit by faith. The Spirit of God breathes new life when one turns from the pride of self and lives for God. Jesus said, *"If any of you want to be my follower, you must stop thinking about yourself and what you want. You must be willing to carry the cross that is given to you for following me."* [4]

To be right with God we must learn to see Him as He is. We must come into the light and be cleansed and washed from our contaminated and inferior thoughts of the Almighty. We must cast away our pride and cling to His saving grace. We must let Him be the God in our mind and heart that He is in all the universe.

When Jesus taught His disciples how to pray, he taught them this very principle: that we are to submit to God and His will on earth and in our lives, depend on Him for all our needs, and seek the forgiveness of God for our sins as we also forgive others when they sin against us. In all things, we are to trust in and lean upon the sufficiency of His grace.

Taking It Home

Before we continue any further, take a moment to ask yourself the most eternally significant question you ever could, "Have I turned from my sin and placed God in His rightful place in my life?" If the answer to this question is "I have not" or "Hmm, I am not really sure?" make that decision today. Jesus said, *"I am light to the world and those who embrace me will experience life-giving light, and they will never walk in darkness."* [5] We cannot know and walk with God or experience His transformational power in our lives until we turn from pride of self and place God in His rightful place in our hearts. The Bible says, *"And now you must repent and turn back to God so that your sins will be removed, and so that times of refreshing will stream from the Lord's presence."* [6]

For those who have turned from sin and trusted in God's saving grace, seek His face yet again with fear and trembling. Many today seek God only after, or at best, alongside their earthly pursuits. We cannot serve two masters. Rather, we must seek him in His holiness and magnificent grandeur where Christ dwells at the Right hand of the Father. We must rid ourselves of ignoble thoughts where Jesus is seen as a nice guy who merely likes people.

Knowledge of God's self-sufficiency safeguards the conscience and eliminates the burden of the soul. Our souls find rest when we trust that God will do His part to provide and preserve. If there be any burden, let it be the joyful one of walking in faith and love unto God as we seek the good of fellow man.

Because God is self-sufficient, His church must remember that God does not need her support. Nervous, flattering pleas, or dominant, strong-arm tactics are not pleasant. God will build His people. God alone will turn hearts back to Him. If we desire to serve may our motive never be to "help God out." God needs no help or defenders. Rather, may our service, dedication, and giving flow out of eternal gratitude for God's incomprehensible mercy and grace that He bestowed upon us when He rescued us from darkness into His marvelous light.

DAY 2

The Self-Sufficiency of God

MAIN IDEA: Without God every facet of life falls apart.

VERSE TO REMEMBER: *"He existed before anything else, and He holds all creation together."* Colossians 1:17 (NLT)

QUESTION TO CONSIDER: In what ways is self-sufficiency hidden in my life?

O Ancient of Days,
You alone are Self-Sufficient;
All things are held together by You,
And without You, nothing can exist;
For You need none except Yourself;
In You do I find my breath,
More than I know.

DAY 3

THE INCOMPREHENSIBILITY OF GOD

To whom can God be compared? How can you describe what he is like?
ISAIAH 40:18 (GNT)

The LORD is great and so worthy of praise!
God's greatness can't be grasped.
PSALM 145:3 (CEB)

It is impossible to fully comprehend God.

Since the very beginning, every man, woman, and child have asked the question, "Who is God, and what is He Like?" The truth is, this question cannot be fully answered except that God is not *exactly* like anything we know. As created beings, we learn by using the raw materials of the mind when venturing into that which is unknown. In other words, we must use that-which-is-not-God to understand who God is and what He is like. And because God cannot be understood or defined by what has been created it is impossible to fully describe or know Him in His fullness.

God Indescribable

In the Biblical accounts whenever the prophets were led by the Spirit before God's Holy Throne, they were perplexed and baffled at what they saw, finding it altogether impossible to describe. In attempts to describe their encounter, they used words and phrases such as "like," "likeness," "as it were" and "the likeness of the appearance" to describe the One who sits on the Throne. Their writings describe being in God's presence as more real than our own reality yet entirely foreign to anything we know or experience here on earth.

In many respects, a bit of obscurity confounds the approach of God. Herein lies one of the many paradoxes of the faith: on the one hand we have an image of God that is seen in Christ, yet on the other hand an unknowable, unapproachable, and imageless God who dwells in abstruseness.

We must deny, therefore, the mental inclination to paint a neat and easy picture of God. In doing so, we will inevitably create an *idol of the mind*. We must also suppress our tendency toward finding security and comfort in a God that we can control. In doing so, we fashion an *idol of the heart*. Idols of the mind and heart are just as offensive and disdainful to God as tangible idols of the hand.

Searching for God

Since human beings were created for God, a profound longing dwells within the heart of man for something that this life can never supply. We yearn to find meaning, satisfaction, security, and purpose; yet, we try to fill those desires through created things — which can never fully satisfy the human soul. Deep within, we all sense that we came from something, somewhere and long to return to our Source. Nevertheless, we wrestle with a sinful nature that alters this desire, subconsciously driving us away from the Source.

If we cannot fully conceive who God is and what He is like, then how shall we be held accountable to know a God who cannot be known? The answer is found in Jesus Christ.

The Bible says that Jesus is the radiance of God's glory and the exact representation of His Being. Through Jesus, God sustains all things by his powerful Word. In opening his Gospel, the Apostle John affirms that in the beginning the Word already existed, that the Word was *with* God, *was* God, and *became flesh* in the Person of Jesus Christ.

The Veil Was Torn

The radiance of God seen through Jesus is even more splendid when one understands what God accomplished for humanity at Calvary. In the Old Testament, we read that God's dwelling on earth was the Holy of Holies — a sacred inner chamber containing the Ten Commandments. Separating the outer parts of the tabernacle and the Holy of Holies was a veil 60 feet high and three inches thick. The veil served as a reminder to Israel of their separation from God because of their sins. Because the Holy of Holies was where God dwelt, man was forbidden to enter. Only once per year could the penitent High Priest enter after sacrificing a bull on the altar. As sacred as the Holy of Holies was, the Bible teaches us that the tabernacle was a temporary dwelling of God among His people and the practice of animal sacrifice was insufficient to forgive sins. The tabernacle served as a mere shadow of what was to be fulfilled through the Messiah, Jesus Christ, for at the very moment Jesus died on the cross, the Bible tells us that veil in the temple was torn in two from top to bottom. This tear represented God's permanent removal of the dividing wall that once separated human beings from God. The Bible says, "*For he has dedicated a new, life-giving way for us to approach God. For just as the veil was torn in two, Jesus' body was torn open to give us free and fresh access to him!*" [1]

Therefore, the dwelling place of God no longer is in a building made by human hands, but within the temple of our heart. The Bible says, "*Surely you know that you are God's temple and that God's Spirit lives in you!*" [2] Through Jesus, our sin was permanently forgiven once and for all. On the cross Jesus said, "*It is finished!*" [3] and because of this we may now enter confidently and boldly into the holiness of God's presence through the blood Jesus shed. The Bible says, "*...we have boldness through him, and free access as kings before the Father because of our complete confidence in Christ's faithfulness.*" [4]

Taking It Home

While it is impossible to fully comprehend God, we can, by faith in Christ and love for God, come boldly before God's Holy presence and know that we are loved and set free.

DAY 3

The Incomprehensibility of God

MAIN IDEA: I can know God even if I can't understand Him.

VERSE TO REMEMBER: *"The LORD is great and so worthy of praise! God's greatness can't be grasped."* Psalm 145:3 (CEB)

QUESTION TO CONSIDER: Do I love God and know the Holy Spirit who resides within me?

O God, who can describe Your fullness?
Incomprehensible, unfathomable, inexplicable;
Yet by the cross, Your Holy Blood was shed,
The barrier removed, my sacrifice bled,
The Holy of Holies, may I now behold,
The great mystery, freedom bought for Me.

DAY 4

THE INFINITY OF GOD

Can you discover the limits and bounds of the greatness and power of God?
JOB 11:7 (GNT)

How great is our God! There's absolutely nothing his power cannot accomplish, and he has infinite understanding of everything.
PSALM 147:5 (TPT)

God is without limit and immeasurable.

The infinity of God is one of the most challenging attributes to understand. The fact that something is limitless and immeasurable is completely beyond comprehension. Everything we know has a beginning, an end, or a limit. God exists outside of this. If we could conceive of His greatness, then He would be less than our own minds; therefore, He would not be God. No language, statement, or idea can grasp the infinitude of God.

Measurement is a means by which human being account for things — describing height, depth, length, weight, limitations, and imperfections. Height and depth describe the upward or downward distance from a given level to a fixed point; length the measure of a dimension or a plane; and weight a system of units for heaviness or mass. Limitations, the boundary or restrictions of a person, place, or thing. Imperfections the defects, weaknesses or incompleteness of a person, place or thing. All these definitions describe the concrete or abstract realities which are the means in which we judge the works of the Creator's hands, but these cannot apply to the Creator.

Because God is infinite everything that flows from Him is infinite as well. When God loves, He loves immeasurably. When God forgives, His forgiveness knows no bounds. When God demonstrates His grace, justice, kindness and mercy, He does so perfectly and infinitely.

Sharing in God's Life

Since we are made in the image of God, and were created to be with God in eternity, we too will share in limitless years. Unlike God, we are created beings with a beginning; however, like God, our soul will have no end.

For those who are in Christ, we share God's own life and will share infinitude with God. Time on earth will be the closest to hell we ever knew, for soon we shall rise to be with God forevermore. For those who are not in Christ, endless time will mean separation from God in consuming fire. Time on earth will be the closest to heaven they ever knew. While this is a sobering thought, the Bible makes this abundantly clear, "*Then he will punish those who do not know God and who do not obey the Good News about our Lord Jesus Christ. Those people will be punished with a destruction that continues forever. They will be kept away from the Lord and from his great power.*"[1]

A Prophecy Yet to be Fulfilled

Throughout the centuries, the church's universal witness has always been, *"For God so loved the world that he gave his one and only Son, that whoever believes in him shall not perish but have eternal life."*[2] For the church, the latter half of this verse remains a mystery to be seen and prophecy yet to be fulfilled. Some glorious day, when the trumpet sounds, those who believe will be raised to live forever. For those who are in Christ, God's infinite power dwells within us by the Holy Spirit. The Bible says, *"Does the Spirit of the one who brought Jesus back to life live in you? Then the one who brought Christ back to life will also make your mortal bodies alive by his Spirit who lives in you."*[3] In view of the resurrection unto eternal life, the Christian mindset has always been in accordance with the apostle Paul. Though he had yet to experience the life to come, he continued to press onward in Christ. Paul looked forward with great anticipation to partaking in both the sufferings of Christ and the future resurrection. Though he had not already obtained this or arrived at his goal, Paul boldly pressed on to take hold of that for which Christ Jesus took hold of him — the salvation of His soul.[4]

Taking It Home

What bearing, then, should the powerful truth of God's infinite nature impress upon our life?

First, we ought to stand in awe of God's infinite nature for God is bigger, greater, and more powerful than we will ever comprehend.

Second, true faith in an infinite God could never be boring or obsolete. Because God is limitless, our lives ought to reflect a powerful confidence that exudes from within us. With God, nothing is impossible, and no circumstance is overwhelming or too difficult.

Third, we must learn to embrace God's infinite grace and mercies toward us. Though at times it may feel like sin towers over as a mountain — that mountain has its limits. Only God is limitless and above all things. Grace, therefore, is greater than all our sin.

Because God is infinite, those who are in Christ share God's own life. Time will run its course and at some point cease to be, but life in Christ will never end. The Bible says, *"And this is the real and eternal life: That they know you, The one and only true God, and Jesus Christ, whom you sent."* [5]

DAY 4

The Infinity of God

MAIN IDEA: Because God is infinite everything that flows from Him is infinite as well.

VERSE TO REMEMBER: *"Can you discover the limits and bounds of the greatness and power of God?"* Job 11:7 (GNT)

QUESTION TO CONSIDER: How does God's infinite nature impact my relationship with Him?

Infinite, unlimited, immeasurable God!
Your Greatness cannot be grasped;
The stars extol Your Name,
Multitudes of heavenly hosts,
And earth sing Your praise;
For without You, life would not be,
And without You, no eternity,
O infinite, God Most High.

DAY 5

THE ETERNITY OF GOD

Your throne was established long ago; you are from all eternity.
PSALM 93:2 (NIV)

Your word is forever, LORD; it is firmly established in heaven.
PSALM 119:89 (ISV)

JUST AS GOD IS LIMITLESS AND MEASURELESS, GOD IS also timeless.

The Bible says, "*...from everlasting to everlasting you are God.*"[1] The timelessness of God can be inferred through the self-existence of God — since God is self-existent, He is therefore timeless. Put another way, since time is a marker that measures the beginning of created existence, God must therefore be timeless since He is uncreated.

As created beings, we view the past as known, the present as uncertain, and the future as unknown. God, on the other hand, has already experienced all our past, present, and future. To God time is simply "now." He sees everything in one view.

It is slightly easier to think about a Creator dwelling at the beginning of time, but to consider One who dwells both at the beginning of time and end of time *simultaneously* is beyond all understanding.

An analogy that may help us understand this truth more clearly is to think of an infinitely extended ocean. That ocean would represent eternity. Now, place a ship in that ocean to represent time. As the bow and stern of the ship begins and ends on that infinitely extended ocean, so time began in and will end in God. Time dwells within God, but God dwells within eternity.

Longing for Eternal Life

There is something about time that rubs us the wrong way. Everything within us cries out for life that will never end yet our experiences tell us different. The Bible says, *"He has put a sense of eternity in people's minds. Yet, mortals still can't grasp what God is doing from the beginning to the end of time."* [2] With time comes the inevitable end of every living creature. When we experience the death of a loved one, we mourn deeply. Somewhere within us there is a soft voice that tells us, "this isn't right!" We mourn because we know death is not right.

We appear to have an inner compass pointing towards something that this this natural world can never offer — life eternal. To be created for eternity but forced to dwell within the confines of time tells us there is more than what meets the eye and a deeper law at work.

Imago Dei

This law is buried within the *Imago Dei* — the image of God in man. Because we are created in God's likeness, we are a soul and have a body. We are given a personality from God that is unique to each one of us that can relate, connect, and interact with others. We also were given the capacity to think, the imaginative ability to envision something and bring that vision to reality, and the emotive facet that allows us to show compassion and experience intimacy with those close to us. We have these abilities because God is a Spirit who is personal, relational, rational, creative, and expresses emotions, such as love.

The characteristics of the *Imago Dei* were meant to be experienced and lived perfectly. Because of the Fall, the image of God in man was devastatingly marred. In Adam's sin, all died spiritually and, our relationship with God was infinitely separated. Humanity's moral purity was substituted by the sinful nature; our personality was fragmented resulting in countless psychological problems; our knowledge became a means toward self-seeking vain glory, and our emotions inclined to fulfill a selfish desire.

Permanence Spoiled

Because of the Fall, the permanence of man was also spoiled. No longer would human beings live forever. Because of their disobedience, God said, *"Now these human beings have become like one of us and have knowledge of what is good and what is bad. They must not be allowed to take fruit from the tree that gives life, eat it, and live forever."*[3] To protect mankind from the potential of living forever in their sinful state, God banished Adam and Eve from the Garden of Eden. Furthermore, He appointed cherubim angels on the east side of the Garden and placed a flaming sword to guard the way to the tree of life.[4]

Although we live in a fallen world, man and woman still retain the characteristics of the *Imago Dei,* though marred, including the sense of permanence that we originally had but lost. In His eternal love, God sent His Son Jesus Christ to die on the cross so that permanence with God could be restored. The Bible says, *"But Christ proved God's passionate love for us by dying in our place while we were still lost and ungodly!"* [5]

Eternal Life and Permanence Now

Eternal life and permanence with God, therefore, is not merely a future event we eagerly look forward to. We can enjoy it in this life *now*.

Permanence with God actually began the very moment we turned from our sin and trusted Jesus Christ. The Bible says we were included in Christ when we heard the message of truth, the gospel of our salvation. When we believed, God marked us with a seal — the promised Holy Spirit — who is a deposit guaranteeing eternal life to come.[6] Receiving the Holy Spirit gives us the assurance that eternal life and permanence with God has already begun!

Taking It Home

Though our experience in this world tells us that things are not right, we can have confidence that we belong to God and our heavenly citizenship is secure. For the Christian, eternal life employs an "already, not yet" factor: on the one hand, we can know and taste the joys of heaven now; while on the other hand, we must remain in our body and in this world until God calls us Home.

The tension between living in this world and longing for permanence compels us to pray with the Apostle Paul in unison and in eager expectation for the eternal life awaiting us, "*We want this dying body to be changed into a living body that lasts forever. It is God Who has made us ready for this change. He has given us His Spirit to show us what He has for us.*" [7]

DAY 5

The Eternity of God

MAIN IDEA: Eternal life and permanence with God began the moment I trusted Jesus Christ.

VERSE TO REMEMBER: *"From everlasting to everlasting you are God."* Psalm 90:2b (NIV)

QUESTION TO CONSIDER: In what ways am I experiencing eternal life now?

Eternal Creator, I worship You;
You made me for permanence,
Yet I am marred by the fall;
Sin had stained, and death did reign;
Yet in Your infinite love, You did save,
Eternal life, and victory over the grave!

DAY 6

THE HOLINESS OF GOD

Holy, holy, holy is the LORD Almighty;
the whole earth is full of his glory.
ISAIAH 6:3 (NIV)

For God saved us and called us to live a holy life. He did this, not because we deserved it, but because that was his plan from before the beginning of time—to show us his grace through Christ Jesus.
2 TIMOTHY 1:9 (NLT)

We know nothing of the Holiness of God.

God is unlike anything we know or could ever fully know. He is infinitely and supremely set apart, incomparable in His Being, and unmatched in His powers. The Holiness of God is unapproachable, incomprehensible, and unattainable in every way. The Holiness of God is purest light and truth. It is an attribute of attributes, for God is completely "other" in every way.

The Bible tells us that before the celestial Throne proceed lightening, thundering, the sound as many waters, and multitudes of cherubim and seraphim angels who day and night sing without rest in rapturous chorus, *"Holy, holy, holy, Lord God Almighty, Who was and is and is to come!"*[1]

When Isaiah was led by the Spirit in the presence of angels before the Throne of the Holy One, he cried out, *"Woe is me, for I am ruined! Because I am a man of unclean lips, And I live among a people of unclean lips; For my eyes have seen the King, the LORD of hosts."*[2] When Job finally met God, he despised of himself before the presence of One so Holy, *"My ears had heard of you but now my eyes have seen you. Therefore I despise myself and repent in dust and ashes."*[3]

Our Depraved State

Unlike Isaiah and Job's supernatural encounters with The Almighty, our natural state is entirely oblivious to God's holiness, for human depravity and God's holiness are precisely opposite. Though we get glimpses of goodness and kindness within us and around us, these are only so because of God's constant goodness, kindness, grace, and mercies that sustain us. Every ounce of good we experience in life ultimately comes from God and God alone. The Bible says, *"Every gift God freely gives us is good and perfect, streaming down from the Father of lights, who shines from the heavens with no hidden shadow or darkness and is never subject to change."*[4]

The truth is we are desensitized to the morally degenerate state we find ourselves in. Our mind, heart, soul, and indeed the world around us are saturated in sin, darkness, and wickedness. For this reason, entering into the presence of One so Holy is impossible. Were it possible to stand before the piercing presence of God's Holiness we would instantly understand, feel, and know the contamination of sin that constitutes every fiber of our natural self.

Until we grasp the grave reality that we are defiled before God, we will never be shaken to the core of our daily, hourly, and moment by moment sins. Even more tragically, we will never fully appreciate or comprehend the gift of God's Son. The church must come to the place where she sees that because God is Holy, He detests sin with an infinite, eternal detestation. The Bible says, *"For the LORD your God is a consuming fire."* [5] Since God is a consuming fire, He burns in white-hot Holy hatred of sin. "The reason we cannot enter into God's presence in our natural state is not because God doesn't want to get "dirty" or become contaminated by our sin. Otherwise Jesus would not have lived among us. Rather, it is because by our very sin nature, we oppose everything that the nature of God is. Because God is a consuming fire, that which is not of Him will be destroyed. Therefore, being before God in a state that is not of God will destroy us in His all-consuming fire." [6]

Contingent Holiness

While God alone is Holy, He imputes a contingent holiness unto His children through faith in Jesus Christ. The Bible says, *"By his will we have been made holy through the offering of the body of Jesus Christ once for all."* [7] Since we are therefore declared by God to be holy, we are to be what He has already declared us to be — holy. We are to think differently and live differently. We are to be in the world but not of the world. The Bible says, "*As it is, you do not belong to the world, but I have chosen you out of the world.*" [8] Martin Lloyd-Jones puts it this way, "Holiness is not something we are called upon to do in order that we may become something; it is something we are to do because of what we already are."[9]

The Impact of Holiness

Our call to holiness is more significant than we may comprehend. We are to be conformed into the image of God — God's purpose from creation — and to reflect His character and nature to the world and the Heavenlies. *Every action, every word, every daily decision we make strikes a chord in eternity.* We must never forget that our words have the power of life or death. Although the tongue is a small part of the body, the Bible says that like the rudder of a ship it has the power to steer the direction of our entire life.[10] The words we say and decisions we make impact our inner spirit as well as others — whether it be toward holiness or destruction.

Taking It Home

In view of the Holiness of God, let the intent of our mind be to walk in the wisdom of Solomon, boldly affirming, "*To fear the LORD is to hate evil.*"[11] Let the desire of our heart be to join the Psalmist in saying, "*My heart says of you, 'Seek his face!' Your face, LORD, I will seek.*"[12]

We must seek to arrive at a place where nothing matters but His Holy presence. All else must drown out as we seek His face alone. All of our cares, desires, and pursuits must decrease to the point where there is but one singular prize — the presence of One who alone is worthy.

We must learn to acclimate our self into a life lead by the Spirit by practicing the presence of God. Through constant meditation upon the Holiness of God, loving what is right, hating what is evil, and growing in acquaintance of the Spirit, we can draw near to the Holiness of God.

Herein lies the common thread of dependence upon God in all things, including nearness in relationship to Him. Since we are incapable of drawing close to God through our own effort, or achieving holiness through our own merit, we must rely on His grace. Brother Lawrence explains, "The world, the flesh, and the devil join forces and assault the soul so untiringly that, without humble reliance upon the ever-present aid of God, they drag the soul down in spite of all resistance. Thus to rely seems hard to nature, but grace makes it become easy, and brings with it joy." [13]

DAY 6

The Holiness of God

MAIN IDEA: God alone is Holy and is making me holy through faith in Jesus Christ.

VERSE TO REMEMBER: *"Be holy, for I am holy."* 1 Peter 1:16b (NIV)

QUESTION TO CONSIDER: How does my life reflect the Holiness of God?

Holy is the Great I AM,
There is none like You,
Brilliant light, indescribable might;
Your presence humbly may I seek,
To know holiness better;
All honor due Your Name.

DAY 7

THE ONENESS OF GOD

Hear, O Israel: The LORD our God, the LORD is one.
DEUTERONOMY 6:4 (ESV)

For the Lord God is one, and so are we, for we share in one faith, one baptism, and one Father. And He is the perfect Father who leads us all, works through us all, and lives in us all!
EPHESIANS 4:5-6 (TPT)

God is One.

While God eternally exists in three distinct Persons — the Father, the Son, and the Holy Spirit — God is one in His Being. The blessed Trinity, though co-equal and co-eternal, do not share the same exact roles, nor are they the same Person. The Father is not the Son or the Holy Spirit, Jesus is not the Father or the Holy Spirit, nor is the Holy Spirit the Father or the Son. In the same manner, the Father and the Holy Spirit were not crucified on the cross, the Son was. The Son did not send Himself to the cross, but the Father. The Holy Spirit is the great Comforter sent from Heaven, not the Father or the Son. The blessed Trinity, though distinct in their personhood, cooperates perfectly as one unified Being.

Oneness in Imago Dei

As an image bearer of God, the *Imago Dei* reveals that we have a mind, a will, and emotions. We each are a soul that also has a body. Although comprised of these aspects, we are one person and each aspect of our make-up affects the other aspects. If the mental or spiritual aspect is weakened, the physical and emotional will be weakened. This is why when we feel physically ill our mind, emotions, and spiritual self also feel vulnerable. Or why our body experiences physical stress when we are mentally or emotionally stressed. The various aspects of our human make-up are indivisible and do not operate independently.

Oneness in Marriage

The sanctity of marriage was also designed to reflect the oneness of God, with the husband and wife, though co-equal, having separate roles. The husband, like Christ, is the head of the household just as Christ is the head of the church. The Bible says, "*The husband provides leadership to his wife the way Christ does to his church, not by domineering but by cherishing.*"[1] The role of the husband carries tremendous responsibility before God. As the head he is responsible for how he loves and leads his wife — with integrity of heart and tenderness of spirit — encouraging her to be the best version of herself. The role of the wife is not any lesser because, biblically-speaking, she is not the head of the household. In many respects, the wife is the adhesive that holds the family unit together and designed by God to be a nurturer of the family — just as the church is designed to nurture and build each other up in the faith. Though comprised of different roles, the husband and wife are a united team that reflect the oneness and glory of God.

Oneness in the Church

As Christ's body, we are comprised of many individual members, or parts, yet each one is uniquely gifted spiritually. Though functionally different from one another, we cannot operate independently. We are one and called to work toward building one another up in love. Simply put: our faith cannot grow and blossom independently from the church. The spiritual life was never meant to be lived out individually with just yourself, God, and the Bible. You are part of Christ's body, His church, and an integral part of the family of God.

Unfortunately, many today see Christianity as a personal, private faith and remain isolated from God's family. They prefer to keep their faith private and not public, and as such, stunt their spiritual potential and miss out on the richness of fellowship that God's family brings.

Our Struggle for Unified Balance

It is a struggle for our natural mind to find balance — a struggle that applies not just to how we view our self but also in marriage and with the body of Christ.

As one person with many aspects, we tend to over-emphasize one or two aspects of our human make-up to the neglect of others. It is difficult to find balance in taking care of our self physically, mentally, spiritually, emotionally, and relationally. Most of us do well in two of three of these aspects but not all of them. We may have seasons where we hit a good stride but inevitably fall back into a rut of imbalance. It takes discipline and hard work to achieve consistent balance.

The same is true for marriage. It is difficult enough to find balance with oneself, let alone in relationship with a spouse. If our life is imbalanced chances are that our marriage will be as well. We offer our best to our spouse when we are striving toward unity within our self and with God.

When it comes to the body of Christ, it is very easy to glorify and over-emphasize certain spiritual gifts in the church over others. The truth is, all gifts are equally essential for the church to grow and operate effectively. The pastor or teacher is no more important than the one who works behind the scenes but is lesser known. This is why the Bible describes the church as one body made up of many parts that forms the whole. It is always about the whole, not the parts. If we make it about the parts, we fail to see oneness and are in danger of glorifying those with certain gifts instead of God Himself.

Our Struggle for Unity

Because of the fall, humanity became fragmented: The masterpiece of God's creation — man and woman — were torn from fellowship with God and are no longer united with Him naturally. Consequently, human beings became fragmented in relationship with one another as well. In the natural state, it is easier to become disjointed and more difficult to be unified.

Though declared holy, individual Christians and the church as a whole still wrestle with the sinful nature. Yet, we have something the world does not have — the Holy Spirit and God's Word. Both are gifts from God to help equip and strengthen us toward greater unity within our own life, our marriages, and the church. The Bible says, *"Live in harmony by showing love for each other. Be united in what you think, as if you were only one person."*[2]

Taking It Home

We are incapable of truly loving without God, especially within marriage. The Bible says that husbands are to love their wives as Christ loves the church and gave Himself up for her. In the same manner, wives are to respect their husbands. The truth is both husbands and wives need love and respect yet experiencing consistent love-respect is impossible since both are imperfect. The guiding presence of the Holy Spirit empowers both husband and wife to live above their natural capacity through applying the love of God toward each other — sacrificially, unselfishly, and generously.

When it comes to the God's people, we must remind our self that God is not Christianity. Church history, like everything else, is filled with high points, low points, and everything in between. Only God Himself is perfect. Some may doubt the imperfections of the church, but they must remember that the body of Christ, like marriage, is comprised of imperfect people seeking to live perfectly. We all wrestle with the sinful nature which will continually be our reality in our present state. As such, we must learn to supply ample grace toward one another as we strive to build each other up until we reach eternal unity. In doing so, we reflect the oneness of God to the world — a oneness that brings God great glory and is a powerful witness.

DAY 7

The Oneness of God

MAIN IDEA: The Holy Trinity are perfectly united in Being and share the same attributes as one God.

VERSE TO REMEMBER: *"Hear, O Israel: The LORD our God, the LORD is one."* Deuteronomy 6:4 (ESV)

QUESTION TO CONSIDER: In what ways do I need to align myself in unity with God so that I might achieve greater unity with those around me?

O God, You are One,
Infinite attributes, One Divinity;
Unity, love, and grace,
These You require of me,
Living as one, perfect harmony.

DAY 8

THE HOLY TRINITY

Therefore go and make disciples of all nations, baptizing them in the name of the Father and of the Son and of the Holy Spirit.
MATTHEW 28:19 (NIV)

The amazing grace of the Master, Jesus Christ, the extravagant love of God, the intimate friendship of the Holy Spirit, be with all of you.
2 CORINTHIANS 13:14 (MSG)

God is three-in-one and one-in-three.

While the Bible never uses the word "trinity," the term encapsulates the divinity of God portrayed throughout the Bible. God eternally exists in three Divine Persons: The Father, The Son, and The Holy Spirit. These three Persons make up the Godhood, are co-equal and co-eternal, have the same nature and attributes, and are worthy of the same worship and adoration.

Function of the Holy Trinity

While the Father, the Son, and the Holy Spirit are all co-existent, co-eternal, and one in divinity, how do they function in relation to one another? One term theologians have used to describe the Holy Trinity's function is the word *economy*. Economy, in this sense, refers to the way their specific roles are ordered.

The Bible teaches us that God the Father creates, God the Son redeems, and God the Spirit is the active Person making us holy. In each order of function, all three Persons of the Godhood are present. While God the Father is preeminently the Creator, the Son and Spirit were also involved. While God the Son is the Redeemer of mankind, the Bible describes the Father and the Spirit as sending the Son to redeem. While the Spirit draws us to the cross and makes us holy, the Father and Son cooperate in this work.

Living in the Love of the Father

The word "God" appears over 4,000 times in the Bible and refers to God the Father. The Father is the fountain of divine love, the source of encouragement we receive in God's Word, the answerer to our prayers, the sender of the Holy Spirit, and the Source of every blessing we receive.

As a loving, gentle, and kind Father, God also disciplines us as His children. When we go through difficult or challenging seasons, we must remember that we have a Heavenly Father that knows everything about us. He only allows us to experience challenges because He loves us and has our best interest in mind. Remember that no situation we encounter in life is too great or difficult for God. In everything let us learn to trust and thank Him for the many blessings we have received — both physical and spiritual. Let us acquire the habit of delighting in His presence as He delights in us as His children and to ask our Heavenly Father to expand our mind and heart to more closely resemble His.

Reflecting the Example of the Son

Jesus pre-existed before time and was with God in the beginning. When we look to the Son, we see the reflection of the unseen God. The Bible says that everything — above and below, visible and invisible, and countless ranks of angels were created by Him and finds its purpose in Him.[1] While Jesus is fully God, He is also fully man. Jesus is not half-God and half-man but both fully and completely. In speaking of Jesus' divinity, the Bible declares, *"For in Christ lives all the fullness of God in a human body."*[2] In speaking of Jesus' humanity, the Bible confirms, *"For there is one God, and there is one mediator between God and men, the man Christ Jesus."*[3]

Through Jesus we have access to the Father and can come confidently and boldly before His Throne. We can have this confidence as a son or daughter because Jesus set us free! As our Savior and Redeemer, Jesus can sympathize with our weaknesses because He has been tempted in every way we have. When we feel weak, Jesus can intercede on our behalf, lavishing us with just the right amount of grace and mercies in our time of need.

Through Jesus we have been brought into God's family and are part of something much bigger than our individual self — the plan of salvation from the beginning of time. This plan is built on the foundation of God's love. As partakers in God's plan, we are now called into a deeper love for God and others. In other words, our lives are to be markedly different as His image bearers. We reflect the character of the Son when we forgive another from the heart, reconcile and restore a broken relationship, make a conscious choice to walk in purity and integrity of mind and heart, and give of our time and resources so we can help others in need.

As a child of God, our calling is a very high calling. In seeking to become like Jesus, everything we say and do leaves an imprint — not only on oneself, but others as well. We must be careful with what we say and do and learn to invest more in our inner relationship with Christ and the inner world of others. It is startling how a human being can achieve so much outwardly yet have a tiny, insignificant soul inwardly; or have a grand, magnificent soul inwardly while having so little outwardly. It does not matter how much one has or does not have, what matters is the condition of the heart.

For many Christians, the message of Jesus has lost its luster. Today's culture has conditioned our mind to place greater excitement on newness — whether in the form of additional knowledge, the novelty of a new experience, or an upgraded version of items we already own. Consequently, the truths, experiences, and material blessings we already learned or received can become less exciting. While continual learning and new experiences are a valuable part of life, we must be very careful not to place a higher value on newness over that which we already know or have received. The sinful nature feeds off novelty and constantly craves for more but will never be satisfied. The Bible says, *"Our eyes and our ears are never satisfied with what we see and hear."*[4] May the message of Jesus Christ crucified and risen from the dead always remain fresh and new to our hearts.

Walking in Step with the Holy Spirit

The Holy Spirit is equal to God the Father and God the Son. The Bible says that the Spirit is our Seal, our Counselor and Guide, and the Comforter in our time of need.

When we placed our faith in Jesus Christ, the Holy Spirit brought us from darkness into the light and made his permanent residence within us. By the Holy Spirit, we have received salvation and are sealed as a son or daughter of God. This seal assures us that God abides within us and we belong to Him!

As our Divine Counselor and Guide, the Holy Spirit never leaves us or forsakes us but is with us every moment of the day. The Holy Spirit teaches and instructs in God's truth — helping us understand the character and nature of God. In addition, the Spirit helps guide us to make wise choices that reflect God's character to others.

The Holy Spirit also opens the eyes of our soul to the truth of God. When we are in the wrong and in need of repentance and forgiveness, or simply need clarity, the Holy Spirit leads us into all truth. As a person who has the freedom to choose, we can listen to or ignore the Holy Spirit. When we choose to ignore what the Spirit is trying to teach us or show us, the Bible says we will not be blessed and displease our Heavenly Father. On the contrary, when we choose to listen and heed what the Spirit is wanting to reveal to us, we will be blessed and bring great joy to our Heavenly Father.

When moments of fear, anxiety, doubt, or uncertainty come — and they will — the Holy Spirit will be there to comfort and strengthen your inner being. The comfort the Spirit brings far surpasses anything the world can offer. While this world can offer some comfort in the form of food, shelter, material blessing, and friendship; the comfort the Holy Spirit provides is fundamentally different. The Spirit assures that God is in control, reminds us that God has our best interest in mind, and that He will work out everything in our life toward a greater good.

Taking It Home

The Persons of the divine Godhood couldn't be more formative toward shaping how we see God and live out our faith each day. *Living in the love of the Father*, *reflecting the example of the Son,* and *walking in step with the Holy Spirit* should be at the very center of our daily life.

In many ways, the essence of God's Triune nature defines the very core of our Christian life and identity. Unfortunately, for most today the trinity has become perceived as a dry doctrine reserved for theologians and academics. This couldn't be further from reality! May God grant the church a renewed hunger and fresh insight into applying the foundational truths of God's triune nature once more.

DAY 8

The Holy Trinity

MAIN IDEA: The Holy Trinity is at the center of my relationship with God.

VERSE TO REMEMBER: *"The amazing grace of the Master, Jesus Christ, the extravagant love of God, the intimate friendship of the Holy Spirit, be with all of you."* 2 Corinthians 13:14 (MSG)

QUESTION TO ASK: How do I perceive the trinity interacting in my life?

Blessed Father,

from Your Hand all things;

Blessed Son,

Substitution and Life You bring;

Blessed Holy Spirit,

Comforter and ever-present guide;

Blessed Trinity,

All worship to You I ascribe!

DAY 9

THE IMPECCABILITY OF GOD

As for God, his way is perfect: The LORD's word is flawless.
2 Samuel 22:31 (NIV)

Christ did not sin or ever tell a lie.
1 PETER 2:22 (CEV)

God is perfect in every way.

Because God is holy, self-existent, and self-sufficient, His character and nature is impeccable, every action is faultless, and every Word that flows from His mouth is flawless. The Father, the Son, and the Holy Spirit exist in perfect union and harmony. Were the Holy Trinity to have even a dab of imperfection, the universe and all of creation would inevitably collapse.

Trusting My Heavenly Father

Because God is perfect, we can trust our Heavenly Father. While most earthly parents have a natural desire to give their best to their children, earthly parents still fall short. God the

Father never falls short. Everything that God does is perfect because He is perfect. In every moment and every season of our life, the Heavenly Father is present and fully involved. He never leaves nor abandons us, but is actively watching over us, directing the course of our life. No matter the situation, God will always be there. The Bible says, *"To the fatherless he is a father. To the widow he is a champion friend. To the lonely he gives a family. To the prisoner he leads into prosperity until they sing for joy. This is our Holy God in his Holy Place!"* [1]

Rejoicing in the Perfect Sacrifice of the Son

Jesus was the perfect sacrifice for sin. The Bible says that He committed no sin, nor did He ever tell a lie. Because Jesus is all-powerful, He was not only able to overcome temptation, but also no temptation was able to succumb Him. Being fully God, His divine nature is both untemptable and impeccable. The Bible says, *"For God is not tempted by evil..."* [2] His human nature, on the contrary, was temptable and peccable. When Jesus' two natures united into one individual existence by the incarnation, His impeccable divine nature overcame his human nature.

The clash between both of Jesus' natures is most clearly portrayed in two stories; one at the beginning of Jesus' ministry and one at the end. In both instances we get glimpses into the vulnerability of Jesus' humanity as it interacted with His divinity.

In commencing His ministry, Jesus spent forty days in the wilderness fasting and praying. Knowing that Jesus was the perfect Lamb of God, Satan attempted to thwart God's plan of salvation. He knew that the human side of Jesus was weakened through fasting and that there was no food readily available. If Satan was going to take out God's plan of salvation before it began, this was his chance. Satan tempted Jesus with food and anything else He wanted in exchange for Jesus' worship. Though He was incredibly weakened in His flesh, Jesus resisted Satan's temptation and remained true to the Father. Philip Yancey captured the implications of this all-important moment at the beginning of Jesus' ministry, "Jesus' resistance against Satan's temptations preserved for me the very freedom I exercise when I face my own temptations. I pray for the same trust and patience that Jesus showed."[3]

At the completion of Jesus' ministry, the anguish of the cross was too much for the human side of Jesus to bear. Knowing that He was about to satisfy the Father's eternal wrath for our sins and that of the world, Jesus was in tremendous agony. As He prayed earnestly to the Father, His sweat fell to the ground like drops of blood as He cried out in a loud voice, *"Father, if you are willing, please take this cup of suffering away from me. Yet I want your will to be done, not mine."*[4] Because of Jesus' obedience to the point of death, God, who is rich is kindness, is able to forgive all our sins. The Bible says, *"Since we are now joined to Christ, we have been given the treasures of redemption by his blood — the total cancellation of our sins — all because of the cascading riches of his grace."*[5]

Obeying the Spirit of Truth

The Holy Spirit is the Spirit of truth and proceeds from the Heavenly Father. Because the Holy Spirit is the Spirit of truth, He is therefore impeccable; for truth does not contain error. Part of the Holy Spirit's job is to guide us into God's truth.[6] Because God's ways are perfect and His Word is flawless,[7] we can trust the Holy Spirit's guidance in our life is sincere.

The Enemy opposes the Holy Spirit and wants to distract us from God's truth and will use anything to preoccupy our mind

— especially when we are feeling weak. Because Satan does not want us to obey the Spirit, we must be alert. Far too many profess faith in Jesus Christ but never spend time listening to the Spirit and obeying God's Word. How will we ever overcome lies and temptation when we are weak if we are not regularly spending time being strengthen by the Spirit and God's truth?

In the wilderness when Jesus was tempted by Satan, Jesus answered Satan's mendacities by declaring truth, "*...man does not live on bread alone but on every word that comes from the mouth of the LORD.*"[8] Like Jesus, may we learn to deny lies and temptation by remaining in the truth of God's Word — regularly.

Taking It Home

While God is perfect, our experience tells us there is much that is imperfect about the world around us. We know that no matter how beautiful and striking God's creation is to the human eye that we still live in a fallen world. We struggle with our own deficiencies, the imperfections of others, and a human experience filled with disappointment. When we feel overcome by these moments, we must remember that we can trust our Heavenly Father — even if life does not make sense. We may not always see God's Hand at work, but we can trust that He loves us and is working out His perfect plan. The Bible says, "*Trust the LORD completely, and don't depend on your own knowledge. With every step you take, think about what he wants, and he will help you go the right way.*"[9]

Let us develop the habit of delighting continually in the perfect sacrifice of the Son. If Jesus Himself wasn't perfect or failed to complete His mission, we would still be lost in our sin. No matter what experiences life throws at us, nothing can take away our salvation! Not only so, but because Jesus was sinless and lived perfectly, we can have the confidence that His sacrifice was enough to forgive us and that the cross is God's one and only way to be forgiven. For if there were another way why would Jesus have had to suffer His darkest hour?

We must cultivate the repetition of moment-by-moment yielding to the voice of the Holy Spirit, the Spirit of truth. Through the help of the Spirit who lives within us, we are to daily crucify sinful attitudes, transform our way of thinking, guard our tongue, and love others from the heart. By the Spirit, let us strive to become what we have already been declared to be — holy. The Bible says, "*For by one offering he has perfected for all time those who are made holy.*"[10] When we feel as if we blew it and messed up, or struggle with habitual sin, God does not see us differently. Too many Christians live their entire life beating themselves over the head with the stick of shame and guilt. We must learn to put the stick down. If God has declared us holy, then we must believe it! Grace and forgiveness are only taken advantage of if we become apathetic about our faith. If we are wrestling with sin yet striving toward God, our heart is in the right place.

Even so, we must be okay knowing that we will never obtain perfection in this life. Perfectionism is an idol that places the pursuit of our own faultlessness over everything else, including God. It seeks to obtain acceptance through our own merit, an impossible pursuit. We must learn to be okay with being imperfect while striving to be perfect — not in order to be loved, but because we already are.

As beloved sons and daughters, may we learn to *trust our Heavenly Father*, *have confidence that we are forgiven by the Son*, and *seek to obey the Spirit of Truth*. In doing so, we will find greater freedom and blessing than we could imagine.

DAY 9

The Impeccability of God

MAIN IDEA: Because God is perfect, I can trust Him, always.

VERSE TO REMEMBER: "*For by one sacrifice he has made perfect forever those who are being made holy.*" Hebrews 10:14 (NIV)

QUESTION TO ASK: In what ways do I need to become more like Christ?

O God, You are impeccable in nature,
Your acts and roles are faultless,
And Thy Word is flawless;
By Your perfect sacrifice,
May I know salvation,
May I know Your Name.

DAY 10

THE TRANSCENDENCE OF GOD

For just as the heavens are higher than the earth, so are my ways higher than your ways, and my thoughts than your thoughts.
ISAIAH 55:9 (ISV)

But who is able to build him a house, seeing heaven and the heaven of heavens cannot contain him?
2 CHRONICLES 2:6A (ASV)

God is infinitely and supremely exalted from creation. When we speak of the transcendence of God, we are not concerned with height or distance but the quality of His Being. Because God is Spirit, He is categorically set apart. All things find their existence in God, but God is distinct from all. He fills the universe, but He is not united together with it. He guides and governs all, while remaining independent from the works of His Hands.

It is a struggle for human beings to think upon God and not default to the raw materials of the mind such as time, matter, and the dimensions of space to understand Him. To use an analogy provided by A.W. Tozer: "Forever God stands apart in light unapproachable. He is as high above an archangel as above a caterpillar, for the gulf that separates the archangel from the caterpillar is but finite, while the gulf between God and the archangel is infinite. The caterpillar and the archangel, though far removed from each other in the scale of created things, are nevertheless one in that they are alike created." [1]

Holy Men of Old

Whenever holy men of old stood before the presence of The Almighty, their encounters were very much the same — an overwhelming sense of awe, unworthiness, and trepidation. When Abraham met God, he instantly fell and lay face down on the ground. When Moses encountered the manifestation of God's presence in the burning bush, he was startled and hid his face for fear to look upon the Lord. When Isaiah was led by the Spirit before the Throne of God, he instantly knew His unworthiness and became undone. When Ezekiel encountered the likeness of the glory of the Lord in His vision, he fell facedown before God and was powerless to stand without the Spirit's help. When Daniel was caught up in a vision before the Ancient of Days, he was deeply disturbed in spirit and his face turned pale.

A Hurried, Self-Confident Church

In this hurried, self-confident day and age, does the church reflect the same holy fear before the majesty of God? Have we become so used to "doing church" that God is merely part of our routine? Do we hold the same sense of exaltation for one who is wholly set apart from His creation and worthy of every ounce of our lives?

It is a fascinating thought to consider what the holy men of old would think of the church today were they to walk among us. How would they assess our spiritual climate? Would they find a people that demonstrate a healthy mix of fear and admiration of God, or would they find a church that has become complacent in our faith? Complacency is the deadly sin of self-satisfaction and seeks little to no change of situation or self. Placing our routine, schedule, and way of doing things above God creates the delusion that values comfortable living above all else. Consequently, faith becomes a mere part of one's life, not the wellspring of it.

Taking It Home

In view of God's transcendence and our tendency toward complacency, how should we seek to realign our heart and mind toward God?

First, we must ask God to help us maintain a high view of Him that disrupts every sense of complacency in our thinking, actions, and daily life. Just as holy men of old held high views of God, so too we should maintain high views of God that exalt Him above all things. The Bible says, "*To be wise you must first have reverence for the LORD. If you know the Holy One, you have understanding.*"[2]

Second, let us learn to praise and thank God for the beauty of creation. Other than our salvation, creation is God's greatest gift to us. Because He created the world and everything in it, He is worthy of every ounce of our worship, exaltation, and praise. If God were not transcendent, He would not have the ability to create or sustain the beauty of life.

Third, let us find great confidence and security in the Bible's teaching with regard with future events. Because God transcends time and eternally exists at all times and places simultaneously, He can predict future events with precision. The Bible says, *"Only I can tell you the future before it even happens."*[3] The level of sureness we have comes in direct proportion to the level of trust we place in God and His Word.

Finally, let us learn to worship and thank God once again in awe and holy fear, for He alone has the power to rescue us from the limitations of this life. Because the physical universe is bound by certain laws, everything we experience inevitably comes to an end. Homes fall apart, cars need to be fixed, our bodies will eventually wear out, and even the sun, moon, and stars — in all their splendor — will eventually cease to be. Because God is transcendent, however, He is not bound by the laws of the universe such as entropy. On the contrary, He is the Originator and Orchestrator of them. Through the cross, God secured eternal life that transcends the limitations we experience in this earthly reality. The Bible says that in His infinite love, God promised to us a future life and a reward that will never perish, spoil, or fade. The Kingdom to come will radiate sustenance and unimaginable life. Permanence with God shall be forevermore. Though this earthly life has its limitations and all things come to an end, those who believe in Jesus Christ shall live even though they die, and those who believe shall never die.[4] The Bible says, *"So since we are receiving an unshakable kingdom, let us give thanks, and through this let us offer worship pleasing to God in devotion and awe."*[5]

DAY 10

The Transcendence of God

MAIN IDEA: God is worthy of all my worship, exaltation, and praise; for He alone transcends all things.

VERSE TO REMEMBER: *"For just as the heavens are higher than the earth, so are my ways higher than your ways, and my thoughts than your thoughts."* Isaiah 55:9 (ISV)

QUESTION TO ASK: Do I have a holy, healthy fear of God?

Lord God Almighty,
You are infinitely and supremely exalted;
Categorically set apart!
Holy, Holy, Holy,
Angelic Hosts sing,
All praise and glory do Your Name.

DAY 11

THE IMMANENCE OF GOD

For in him we live and move and have our being.
ACTS 17:28A (NIV)

The LORD is near to all those who call upon Him,
to all who call upon Him in truth.
PSALM 145:18 (MEV)

God is actively present and participating in the details of your life.

While the transcendence of God refers to His distinction *from* creation, the immanence of God refers to His active presence and participation *in* creation. Both attributes are equally and simultaneously true.

Because God is immanent and transcendent, He guides, governs, and provides for all while remaining distinctly and uniquely the Sovereign God over all. There are no instances, no moments, no places where God is not closely involved. From the subatomic, quantum level, to the activities of man, to plants, animals, and sea life, to the innumerable stars and galaxies of the universe; God is ever near and ever present in every detail. The

Bible says, "*Starting from scratch, he made the entire human race and made the earth hospitable, with plenty of time and space for living so we could seek after God, and not just grope around in the dark but actually find him. He doesn't play hide- and-seek with us. He's not remote; he's near. We live and move in him, can't get away from him!*"[1]

The incarnation of Christ through the virgin birth is the ultimate example of God's divine transcendence and immanence united in one. In the Person of Jesus Christ, we see the Holy, transcendent God who took on flesh and made His dwelling among us. Jesus had parents, helped around the house, grew up, attended school, learned a skilled trade, and experienced the same kind of things we do — including the mundane! Indeed, the very name Immanuel means "God with us."

Nearness Through the Son and the Spirit

Because Jesus ascended to the right hand of the Father, we may receive the gift of the Holy Spirit, who is the divine Encourager.[2] By the Holy Spirit we enjoy nearness with God. Though Jesus is presently at the right hand of the Father, He remains actively involved in our lives today as if He never left! When Jesus spoke about all these things to His disciples, He affirmed that we would be one with He and the Father, "*So when that day comes, you will know that I am living in the Father and that you are one with me, for I will be living in you.*[3]

God's ultimate desire for the church is that in becoming like Christ we might reflect His glory to the world as His image bearers. St. Athanasius wrote, "He became what we are so that we might become what he is."[4] Redemption was never for redemption's sake, but to bring glory to the Living God as we shine His light to a dark world. The Bible says, "*We all show the*

Lord's glory, and we are being changed to be like him. This change in us brings more and more glory, which comes from the Lord, who is the Spirit."[5] Transformation ultimately comes by the power of the Holy Spirit who takes out the heart of stone from our body and gives us a new, tender heart.[6] Therefore, the old self is gone and the new self has come. We are a new creation in Christ, everything is fresh and new.[7] The hallmark of being near to God is always a changed life.

God Is Interpersonal

Since God is a Person, He can relate interpersonally. He hears our prayers, rejoices over us, loves us and provides for us. Conversely, we can pray to Him, worship Him, love Him, obey Him, and walk with Him. God is personally aware and cares about every detail of your life. Because Jesus took on humanity, He understands humanity and can sympathize with every struggle and weakness we face because He experienced the same things we do, including the temptations of sin. The Bible says, *"Jesus understands every weakness of ours, because he was tempted in every way that we are. But he did not sin!"*[8]

Unfortunately, many Christians believe that God is constantly disappointed in them or that Jesus cannot relate to humanity since, after all, Jesus was perfect, and they are not. This perspective could not be further from the truth. While God does desire for us to pursue holiness and to become more Christ-like, He is not distant or cold toward His children, nor is He constantly frowning upon our every action. He is Holy, yes, but in His holiness His love toward us is perfect. God truly rejoices over us — more than we know. The Bible says, *"The Lord your God is with you; his power give you victory. The Lord will take delight in you, and in his love he will give you new life. He will sing and be joyful over you."*[9] Learn to see God as both sovereign King who cares about and is actively involved in the details of your daily life — rejoicing over you as He lovingly draws you closer to His heart.

Taking It Home

It is a challenge for some Christians to believe that God is actively present in the details of their life. Why would God care about the details when He has a grand universe to occupy His attention? This is a fair question but one that is very human. Because our mind is finite and has boundaries, we cannot know or pay attention to everything. God is not bound by these restrictions. The Bible says, "*And he pays even greater attention to you, down to the last detail — even numbering the hairs on your head!*"[10]

The fact that God knows us more than we know our self and is actively participating in every detail feel both mystifying and liberating. Every minutiae God is fully aware of and can use toward His good purposes. The Bible says, "*For in him we live and move and have our being.*"[11] God moves in every detail; and every detail serves its purpose.

DAY 11

The Immanence of God

MAIN IDEA: God is actively present and participating in the details of my life.

VERSE TO REMEMBER: *"The LORD is near to all those who call upon Him, to all who call upon Him in truth."* Psalm 145:18 (MEV)

QUESTION TO ASK: How do I see God working in the details of my life?

Ever present God,
You never leave, You never forsake,
Always near, always by my side;
My strength, my source;
In You do I live.

DAY 12

THE OMNIPRESENCE OF GOD

Your Spirit is everywhere I go. I cannot escape your presence. If I go up to heaven, you will be there. If I go down to the place of death, you will be there.
PSALM 139:7-8 (ERV)

Do not I fill heaven and earth?" declares the LORD.
JEREMIAH 23:24B (NIV)

God is everywhere.

The immanence and omnipresence of God are closely related. While the immanence of God refers to His *nearness* and *active presence* in creation, the omnipresence of God refers to His *universal nature* — God is equally present at all places and all times. The word present of course means "here," "near," or "close," and the word omni means "all." God is all-present.

In actuality, the correct way to understand the omnipresence of God is by employing the use of the negation, what God is not: God is not present in all of creation; but, rather, *all of creation is in the presence of God*. For God is infinite but creation is finite.

The World is Spiritual

Because God is omnipresent, we can positively assert that the universe originated by the Spirit, ebbs and flows from the Spirit, and is meaningless and hollow apart from the Spirit. For matter came from Spirit, not Spirit from matter. The Latin term ex nihilo, or, "creation from nothing" captures the essence of this profound theological truth. Scripture affirms, *"Faith empowers us to see that the universe was created and beautifully coordinated by the power of God's words! He spoke and the invisible realm gave birth to all that is seen."* [1] Because matter came from the Spirit, we must remind our self that ultimate reality is not physical but spiritual. The Bible compares our short earthly experience to a mere dream compared to the realness of the spiritual realm.[2] Since our true home is with God for eternity, live in a manner that invests more in what is unseen than what is seen, for what is seen is temporary but what is unseen is eternal.[3]

God Sees and is Fully Aware

The fact that God is present everywhere means He is not only actively participating in creation but sees everything happening within it. Every action, every word, every decision, and the implications of those decisions, God sees — including the moments or seasons of life where we feel abandoned and wonder if God has forgotten you.

Hagar must have felt this way. As a servant of Abraham and Sarah (previously Abram and Sarai), Hagar had an uncertain future and no husband to fend for her or raise a family with. She must have felt alone and wondered whether the God of Abram cared for her or had forgotten her. Because Sarah was barren, in accordance with the customs of those days, Sarai had her servant Hagar conceive of a child with Abram, then force Hagar to give up her child to be considered Sarai's child, Abram's heir. After she conceived, Sarai despised of Hagar, so Hagar fled to the desert to avoid the Sarah's mistreatment. It was there, in the desert and amidst great despair that God appeared to Hagar near a spring and refreshed her spirit by announcing that her son would be called Ishmael, which means *"God hears."* Because God had heard her plea of desperation, Hagar gave God the name *"El Roi,"* meaning *"the God who sees me,"* for God saw her misery and had answered her prayer.

Like Hagar, there will be times where you feel that God has abandoned you, leaving you to fend for yourself. Your future feels uncertain and the present seems precarious. In these moments, when you are tempted to say, "Where is God and does He care for me?" remember Hagar's story and the God who sees you. God sees and knows your circumstance. God will meet you there.

Because God sees and is fully aware, knowledge of God's omnipresence should be a source of great comfort, especially amidst trials and tribulations. Like gold refined by fire, the difficulties we encounter will only refine our faith, making us more holy. While gold is valuable it can still tarnish. As God's children our faith is worth more than gold and will never tarnish.[4] Trials and tribulations, if we allow them, will only refine our character making us more like our Savior.

God is Never Overwhelmed by Prayer

God's omnipresence means He hears our every prayer — even if they occur at different locations at the same time! This is possible since God is eternal and exists outside of time has all of eternity to hear our prayers. As an example, when a pilot or driver behind the wheel have a split second to decide, from

God's perspective He already knew about that moment from all eternity and the prayer that was "quickly thrown up" in a fraction of a second. While this is may be a perplexing concept for us to grasp it is true nonetheless...God's omnipresence and eternality means He is never overwhelmed.

Taking It Home

While the omniscience of God can be a tremendous source of encouragement it is also a sober reminder that someday we will stand before God and give an account for every choice we made in life, including the ones we perceived to be trivial. Everything will be uncovered and laid bare before the eyes of the Lord,[5] including every secret thing.[6] The Bible says, *"For the LORD sees clearly what a man does, examining every path he takes."*[7]

On that Day, not only will those choices will be brought into light, they will also direct our ultimate outcome. For those who have chosen Christ, our verdict will be one that weighs every intent and motive of our heart — an unveiling of what works were and were not done for God. Works stream from the heart and the heart is tied to motive. It is not the works itself that matters but the heart rightly aligned with the Spirit. Though cleansed and forgiven of sin by the cross, believers will still give an account for every facet of our earthly lives.

For those who have chosen to reject Christ, the Word of God plainly states that their judgement will be eternal separation from the Lord's presence. Because God examines all, living as if one will not be held accountable is foolhardy. Just as Adam and Eve hid from God in the Garden when they disobeyed God, it is foolish to try and hid from God today or at judgement for no place exists where God is not present. It is helpful to point out that there is a difference between *factually knowing that Jesus is the Savior* and *fully committing yourself to Jesus as your Savior.* Satan and the demons know who Jesus is, yet they will not be spared eternal punishment. It is not knowing that matters but the heart which has trusted and believed. The Word of God thoroughly discloses this pivotal truth, "*There is no judgment against anyone who believes in him. But anyone who does not believe in him has already been judged for not believing in God's one and only Son.*"[8] The word "belief" and the word "trust" are synonymous in the Greek New Testament and always imply a committed, heartfelt action on behalf of the Christian. If you have believed the heart and mind follow, and therefore one's entire life.

Lastly, the omnipresence of God also serves as a strong underpin for the church. When it comes to ministry and mission, Jesus stated that He would be with His disciples to the very end of the age.[9] No matter where our mission takes us on earth Jesus will be with us. As children of God, our life mission is to join God in redeeming all things through pointing others to the redeeming truth of the cross.

DAY 12

The Omnipresence of God

MAIN IDEA: Because God is omnipresent, He sees everything, is equally present, and fully aware.

VERSE TO REMEMBER: *"For the LORD sees clearly what a man does, examining every path he takes."* Proverbs 5:21 (NLT)

QUESTION TO ASK: How can I live better knowing God sees my every action?

All creation is in Your presence,
The greatest heights, the deepest depths,
Where can I go, for You are there,
Equally present, fully aware.

DAY 13

THE IMMUTABILITY OF GOD

For I am the LORD, I change not.
MALACHI 3:6A (KJV)

Jesus Christ never changes! He is the same yesterday, today, and forever.
HEBREWS 13:8 (CEV)

GOD DOES NOT CHANGE.

When we reflect upon the attributes of God, two self-evident truths stand out. The first is that God cannot be one attribute and not all His other attributes at the same time. The second is that God does not change. Just as God is limitless, measureless, timeless, and faultless, God is also changeless.

Because God is perfectly Holy, He cannot change for the better. God has never been more or less Holy. He is eternally the same. God is all in all, and all that He has been He always will be. Even as we grow and mature in our faith, God does not grow or mature with us, for it is never God who changes in relationship, but we who change as we draw closer to Him.

The world and all creation are constantly changing — from trends that consume popular culture, to the rise and fall of nations and leaders, to the lifespan of the stars in the universe — nothing ever remains fixed. God, however, is forever constant. He is above the eb and flow of the universe, the trends of the world, and eras of nations and leaders. With so much uncertainty and change in the world, the fact that God never changes is truly good news.

Humanity Subject to Change

While laws of nature evoke constant change in our surroundings, change is equally part of our human experience. Since human beings have free will, we have a choice, and these choices may not always be the best ones. We may say one thing and do another, demonstrate positive character one day and negative character the next, forget a promise we made, revise our opinions, or change our entire attitude on a whim.

This is one of the most difficult parts about life. Human beings can endure natural change in our world such as natural disasters, but the pain and suffering caused by ourselves or another human being can be especially difficult to bear.

God is Eternally the Same

Fortunately, God is not like us. Because God is immutable, His character is trustworthy; His faithfulness dependable; and His decisions fully reliable. While there are places in the Bible that seems to indicate God "changes His mind" or "alters His opinion," we must remember that God is eternally sovereign, omniscient, and does not change. How do these apparent contradictions add up? Here are two considerations:

First, *the Bible often uses anthropomorphic means of communicating.* What this means is that scripture often gives God human qualities and characteristics to help bridge the content to the reader to make its concepts more understandable and relatable. The intentional use of this language by the biblical authors provides a helpful bridge since it correlates with how we think and experience reality.

Second, *God cannot be affected by any outside cause other than Himself.* Let's unpack this second concept a little further. What exactly is it that brings about change? The answer is that change ultimately occurs when a cause effects an original composition resulting in a new composition. That is to say, for change to occur there needs to be an outside cause that effects the original object resulting in an entirely new state.

To use an example: If a man demonstrated a humble attitude one day but a proud attitude the next, what actually *caused* this difference? The cause could have been a thought that came into his mind, the flattering words of another that inflated his ego, or something the man did which made him feel exceedingly important. In any case, there was a cause which the man responded to — a thought that came into his mind, thewords from another, or something he did. Because the man has free will, he can choose how he will respond when he encounters any one of these hypothetical causes. Either he will respond with pride, or he will deny the temptation of pride and remain humble of heart.

Because God is immutable, He is not subject to the influence of any outside cause. God's self-existent and self-sufficient nature means He is not affected by, dependent on, or altered by anything other than Himself. God cannot be strong-armed, nor can He be bribed, flattered, or appeased. The Bible says, *"For I am the LORD, I change not."*[1] This is why the Scriptures often compare God to a strong rock. Though, technically, we know that rocks can change their composition over time, they are nonetheless known as a strong, immovable part of creation.

God's Immutability a Source of Assurance and Comfort

For the Christian, the immutability of God is source of assurance and comfort, for we can know that when we come to the Father in prayer, He will always respond in a manner that is consistent with His nature. God will always be an affectionate God that loves justice and hates sin. God will always be merciful, teeming with kindness and overflowing in abundant grace. God will always forgive when we confess our sins to Him. The Bible says, "*From eternity to eternity I am God.*"[2]

Because God is unchangeable, we can experience true joy, peace, security, and comfort. We can cast all our hopes, fears, concerns and dreams upon Him and know that God is not fickle nor subject to whimsical decision making. What a relief!

God's Immutability the Bedrock for Salvation

The immutability of God is also a bedrock for salvation. The gospel never changes, and neither will the Lord Jesus. The Bible says, "*Jesus Christ never changes! He is the same yesterday, today, and forever.*"[3] Consequently, the good news of Jesus Christ becomes even more commanding when we proclaim the unchangeable nature of God. Because Jesus is the same yesterday, today, and forever, His love towards humanity remains the same. The cross is forever solidified as the divine act of God's eternal love for humankind. King David said, "*He alone is my rock, my deliverance, and my high tower; nothing will shake me.*"[4] The truth that God never changes is a powerful message for a world used to disappointment, heartache, and let down. God's infinite love toward humanity is not capricious nor does it last but a season.

Taking It Home

God's will for our life is that our character become conformed to the image of His Son. Character is developed through consistently doing the right things — over and over. It takes discipline to break a habit. We can pray every day and ask God for a changed heart, but until we exercise our heart in that direction, we will never experience transformation in our lives. The Bible says that we are to work out our salvation with fear and trembling.[5] This does not mean that salvation is earned through doing good works, for salvation comes by grace alone through faith alone. Rather this verse means we are to regularly examine our heart and attitude before God candidly:

> *Do my actions match my professed faith?*
>
> *Does my love for God reflect itself in the way I treat others?*
>
> *Does my character match the consistency and trustworthiness of the Savior?*

While we do not oversee our own sanctification (the Holy Spirit does) we are to cooperate with the Spirit in this work as we seek to consistently reflect God's character to the world.

DAY 13

The Immutability of God

MAIN IDEA: God is eternally the same in His character and nature.

VERSE TO REMEMBER: *"For I am the LORD, I change not."* Malachi 3:6a (KJV)

QUESTION TO ASK: In what ways do I need to become more consistent in my character?

O God, You change not,

Eternally the same,

Unchangeable, unalterable,

Lord God unmovable;

Yesterday, today, and forever,

You shall always be,

A strong rock in which I trust.

DAY 14

THE OMNISCIENCE OF GOD

...for the LORD searches all hearts, and understands every intent of the thoughts.
1 CHRONICLES 28:9B (NASB)

Lord, you know everything there is to know about me. You perceive every movement of my heart and soul, and you understand my every thought before it even enters my mind.
PSALM 139:1-2 (TPT)

God knows everything.

Nothing has been, will be, or could be that God does not know. Because God is infinite, His knowledge is infinite. Because God is self-existent, His knowledge had no beginning. Because God is impeccable, His knowledge knows all things perfectly and equally. Because God is holy and transcendent, His knowledge is categorically set apart. God has always possessed knowledge of eternity past and eternity future — including the infinite multiplicity of potential realities that could have been or may be.

How does this relate to the language of the Old and New Testament that seems to indicate that God "learns"? When the

Bible uses phrases such as "when God learned" or "when God saw" it does not imply that God discovered something He did not previously know. Instead the writers are employing the same use of anthropomorphic language in the narrative — the attribution of human qualities in describing God to be more understandable and relatable to the reader.

Identity Found in God

God's omniscience and impeccability means He possesses not only the ability to know all things perfectly, but Himself perfectly. The fact that God possess complete knowledge of Self and is fully Self-aware has profound implications on how humanity views itself — for it is impossible to fully understand ourselves, yet we were created by God who knows Himself fully and completely. As such, knowing and understanding oneself may actually be more challenging than knowing and understanding God since our very existence is derived from God. And since our very existence is derived in God, our purpose and identity are also found in Him. Therefore, generally speaking, the more we seek to understand, know, and draw closer to God the more we will come to a knowledge of ourselves.

Specifically, the true you is identified in Christ. The Bible says, *"Your crucifixion with Christ has severed the tie to this life, and now your true life is hidden away in God in Christ."*[1] Due to the perplexing nature of this world, our identity is often difficult to perceive. Since this life was never meant to be our permanent home but often feels like it is, we have trouble viewing ourselves clearly. It is easier to identify with our surroundings and less easy to identify with something we cannot see, touch, hear, and experience tangibly. Nevertheless, in Christ, the true you is known by God as a child of the King — holy, loved, righteous, and redeemed. You are a co-heir in God's eternal Kingdom and more than a victor. By the Holy Spirit you have power to live a godly life, you can have infinite peace, joy, and lasting satisfaction. Because you are forgiven and free, you have what the world desperately searches for but will never find — rest for one's soul. The words of Saint Augustine summarize well the human soul's deep longing for meaning, purpose, and identity, *"Thou hast made us for Thyself, O Lord, and our heart is restless until it finds its rest in Thee."*[2]

Taking It Home

In view of the omniscience of God, what practical implications are there for the believer?

First, let us view the omniscience of God is an illuminating light. He knows our life more than we do and the path in front of us, including times of turmoil. The Bible says, *"Don't be afraid, I've redeemed you. I've called your name. You're mine. When you're in over your head, I'll be there with you. When you're in rough waters, you will not go down. When you're between a rock and a hard place, it won't be a dead end - Because I am GOD, your personal God, The Holy of Israel, your Savior."*[3] Because the arrow of time moves forward and not backward, future events and outcomes are uncertain. Therefore, we must learn to give up want of control and embrace God instead. The Bible says, "...*for we walk by faith, not by sight."*[4] Because God alone knows our future, all our experiences, every encounter, and every situation are already fully known.

Second, because God know everything, we can know that He's got it. As sons and daughters of faith, we must not be afraid to regularly ask the Father for perspective and peace. Instead we should come boldly before His presence. Even if we pray the same prayer a million times over God will never become annoyed. We must learn to be authentic with God! Over and over in the Psalms we read of the honest and very candid conversations David had with God. Sometimes he rejoiced. Other times he was angry, wept, or lamented. Still other times David expressed fear, concern, and even doubt. Being honest with God has a way of cleansing and refreshing the soul. We must learn to be authentic while also thanking God for what He has done. The Bible says that when we do this heavenly peace will come upon us and guard our mind and heart.[5]

Lastly, we must view the omniscience of God as a beautiful truth that revives the soul. To know that we are fully known by God yet fully loved is indescribable. God knows every detail of our lives, including the things we are not proud of, yet He loves us with an everlasting love. King David wrote, *"Every single moment you are thinking of me! How precious and wonderful to consider that you cherish me constantly in your every thought!"*[6] God cannot love you any more or any less. His love is truly without bound.

DAY 14

The Omniscience of God

MAIN IDEA: God knows everything, including all possible outcomes.

VERSE TO REMEMBER: *"...for the LORD searches all hearts, and understands every intent of the thoughts."* 1 Chronicles 28:9b (NASB)

QUESTION TO ASK: Do I have deep, inner peace knowing God knows everything about my life?

Lord, You know all things,
You know my coming and going,
You know my thoughts and actions beforehand,
Nothing escapes Your all-encompassing knowledge;
May I find peace, serenity, and joy in You,
To be fully known yet fully loved,
Beyond description.

DAY 15

THE PROVIDENCE OF GOD

So we are convinced that every detail of our lives is continually woven together to fit into God's perfect plan of bringing good into our lives...

ROMANS 8:28A (TPT)

You intended to harm me, but God intended it for good to accomplish what is now being done, the saving of many lives.

GENESIS 50:20 (NIV)

GOD MAKES ALL THINGS WORK TOGETHER FOR THE greater good.

Because God is all-present, all-knowing, and all-powerful, He can fulfill His divine purpose. The word providence comes from the Greek word *pronoeo*, which means "to foresee," "to have regard," "to provide," and "to perceive." In essence, God can look ahead or provide in advance. While the providence of God can be understood as the divine *acts of God* by which He sovereignly fulfills his purposes, God's providence is also *something true of Him* — God is providential.

The Bible says that God is sovereign which means that no plan of His can be changed, altered, or prevented. In His infinite wisdom, God is able to move in and through man's choices yet still fulfill His divine plans. Herein lies another paradox: somehow, someway, God's sovereignty and man's free will works together to achieve God's perfect will. While God can work through deeds that are both good and evil, *God does not cooperate with the evil that is in the deed, but He can still use the deed itself.*

Regarding God's relationship to evil, the Bible affirms, "*…for God cannot be tempted by evil, and He Himself does not tempt anyone.*"[1] In other words, evil remains under God's authority for He incapable of being tempted by evil (nor does He tempt human beings to do evil).

Although the providence of God may appear to be a clandestine reality enshrouded in mystery, it is actually a foundational truth we experience every day. God is intricately involved our life. From major life-changing events, to the seemingly trivial, to the monotonous, God can use anything and everything to achieve His greater purposes.

From Genesis through Revelation, the Bible is chock-full of stories that reveal the providential Hand of God. Let's look at three stories in particular: Joseph, the youngest son of Jacob, whom God raised up to save his generation and generations to come; an unnamed woman in the gospels, through whom Jesus demonstrated His salvation and grace; and the Apostle Paul whom God prepared from youth to spread the gospel.

Joseph in Egypt

In the book of Genesis, we read of a confident young man named Joseph. His older brothers were jealous of him since their father Jacob favored and sheltered him. To add insult to injury, Joseph boasted to his older brothers that they would someday bow to him — a prophecy he received in a dream. When Joseph's brothers could no longer stand the favoritism, they devised a scheme to sell Joseph to a group of Ishmaelites who were passing by on their way to Egypt. To frame this act, they kept the robe their father, Jacob, gave Joseph and dipped it in blood so that it appeared that Joseph was attacked by a wild animal.

Though Joseph would suffer betrayal at the hand of his own family, be sold as a slave to Potiphar, and then framed by Potiphar's wife and thrown into prison, God was with Joseph. His guiding providence never left him, even during mistreatment and betrayal.

In His wisdom, God allowed Joseph to encounter loss after loss to shape Joseph's character for a bigger purpose. God eventually brought Joseph out of prison and raised him to second in command to Pharaoh. In this position Joseph received prophetic direction to set aside seven years of grain for it was revealed that seven years of famine would come. When the famine came, the dream Joseph received in his youth would finally come true, for his older brothers would arrive in Egypt along with their father, for the famine had devastated all the land. In confronting his brothers kneeling before him, an older, wiser Joseph would empathetically profess, *"You intended to harm me, but God intended it for good to accomplish what is now being done, the saving of many lives."*[2] The saving of many lives included preserving the lineage of Jesus, the Savior of the world.

An Unnamed Woman

The Gospels we read an account of an unnamed woman, who demonstrated love for her Savior. In coming to Jesus with an alabaster jar full of expensive perfume, she proceeded to pour the perfume on Jesus' head. To the disciples and all who were present, this seemed like a total waste, for the perfume could have been sold and the proceeds given to the poor. To the woman, however, this was a sacrificial gesture expressing her gratitude for the extravagant love of God.

Though her act was simple, the woman's genuine expression of love turned into a prophetic moment as Jesus announced, *"You can be sure that wherever in the whole world the Message is preached, what she has just done is going to be remembered and admired."* [3] Her story is still told today.

The Apostle Paul

In the book of Acts, we read about the apostle Paul, formerly known as Saul, who was a violent persecutor of the church and believed his zeal for exterminating Christians was honoring God. As Saul neared Damascus to oversee further persecutions, a blinding light from heaven suddenly flashed and he fell to the ground. As Jesus confronted Saul from the light, He confirmed that he would be no longer be called Saul but Paul, for he was God's chosen instrument to bring the gospel to the nations. Up to that moment, Saul's entire life had been a preparation for the gospel — though he did not know it at the time. Not only would his extensive training and breadth of knowledge of the Scriptures prepare him for the spreading the gospel but also his natural zeal to serve God. In His sovereignty, God providentially orchestrated every single event in Paul's former life to prepare him for his new life as an apostle. Through Paul, we now have seventeen books of the Bible.

Countless times, over and over in God's Word we read how the Hand of God providentially guided the course of history. Just as God was at work through Joseph's betrayal, a woman's sacrificial gesture of love, and Paul's extensive training and misplaced zeal, God has always been at work in your life — even when you could not perceive what He was doing. Like an intricately woven tapestry, God is weaving the details of your life together to form a beautiful whole. The Bible says, *"So we are convinced that every detail of our lives is continually woven together to fit into God's perfect plan of bringing good into our lives..."*[4] While your vantage point only sees the back of the tapestry — an oft perceived random mess — God sees the back and the front in one single view with the final result of your life being God's masterpiece.

The most definitive act of God in human history was the death and resurrection of Jesus Christ. In His sovereign wisdom, God allowed sinful men to condemn His sinless Son. From the eyes of the disciples, the cross appeared to be a complete disaster. Their hopes were dashed, their dreams scattered, and their mission had come to a painful end. The darkest day in history; however, would become the illuminating light of God's providence, for by the cross God would reconcile a lost, broken, and hurting world to Himself.

Taking it Home

Just as Joseph's betrayal seemed unfair, the unnamed woman's sacrificial gesture seemed unnecessary, Paul's extensive training and zeal seemed like a waste, and the crucifixion seemed like sheer tragedy, there are plenty of moments in our life that seem unfair, unnecessary, wasteful, or tragic. In those moments, remember that though we cannot comprehend everything, God has a great plan. As God's children, we must learn to rest in the truth of His providence. The Bible says, *"For what seems to be God's foolishness is wiser than human wisdom, and what seems to be God's weakness is stronger than human strength."*[5] God knows what He is doing. God can weave every single detail of your life together. Do you believe this?

The final course of history will someday culminate with the coronation of Christ. When the times have reached their fulfillment and this age has run its course, God will bring unity to all things, including things in heaven and on earth under one sovereign rule. On that day, the foresight of God will shine brighter than the noonday sun, and the things that didn't make sense, *couldn't* make sense will make sense. The Bible says, "*Now we see things imperfectly, like puzzling reflections in a mirror, but then we will see everything with perfect clarity."*[6]

DAY 15

The Providence of God

MAIN IDEA: God can work through any situation for His greater good.

VERSE TO REMEMBER: *"So we are convinced that every detail of our lives is continually woven together to fit into God's perfect plan of bringing good into our lives."* Romans 8:28a (TPT)

QUESTION TO ASK: In view of God's providence, how can I apply greater perspective to life?

O God, Your purposes reach higher than the heavens,
Your infinite knowledge and sovereign power,
Work out all things for my greater good,
No time, experience, or effort is a waste;
Endless king, You watch over me,
I rejoice in Your wisdom.

DAY 16

THE OMNIPOTENCE OF GOD

I am the LORD God of all humanity. Nothing is too hard for me.
JEREMIAH 32:27 (GW)

For with God nothing shall be impossible.
LUKE 1:37 (KJV)

ONE CANNOT BEGIN TO COMPREHEND THE POWER OF Almighty God.

No other being has unlimited capability and energy. While God grants others power and influence, the authority still belongs to Him. God gives but He does not give away, for all power comes from God and returns to God.

The universe is perhaps the most astounding testimony to the power of God. While the observable universe is estimated to be 92 billion light years from one end to the other, the actual universe is estimated to be immeasurably larger than one can fathom. In fact, many astrophysicists believe that the actual universe is to the observable universe as the observable universe is to…an atom. This is a scale of unthinkable proportions. With what we can merely observe, if you put a grain of sand on your finger and hold it up to the sky, the infinitesimal patch of sky the tiny grain blocks out contains 10,000 galaxies, with each galaxy containing 100 billion stars.[1] The number of stars in this tiny patch of sky alone far outnumber the grains of sand on earth. All of this was spoken into existence by the power of God's Word. Yet, the creation account in Genesis gives credit to God's incalculable formation of the universe with a single phrase, *"He also made the stars."*[2] One cannot begin to grasp the kind of energy and power behind all of this. If the Creator can speak the universe into existence without exhausting *any* power, what must *He* be like?

Omnipotence Seen Through Creation

The Bible says that from the very beginning, God's eternal powers have been on display and plain for all to see. Every man, woman, and child know deep within that there is an intelligent Creator and that He must possess unlimited power. Though we cannot see Him or fully recognize Him, all creation testifies to the eternal power of His Being. The Bible says, *"By taking a long and thoughtful look at what God has created, people have always been able to see what their eyes as such can't see: eternal power, for instance, and the mystery of his divine being. So nobody has a good excuse."*[3]

Not only are God's powers on display through creation, they also attest to God's very existence. The fact that there even *is* a universe necessitates a cause. To say that there is no God is to say there is no cause. If there is no cause and mass-energy always existed, where did the mass-energy originate? There is nothing irrational about an eternal, omnipotent Being, but there is something irrational about mass-energy created out of nothing, or mass-energy always existing because both violate the laws of causality. Therefore, there had to be an original cause, and that cause *must possess all-power.*

The *Dunamis* of God

For those who have placed their faith in Christ, the omnipotence of God is an astonishing source of inner power. The Greek word for power in the New Testament is *dunamis* and refers to "inherent ability," "might," "strength power," "moral power," or "miraculous power." Regardless of what each day brings, the believer can experience the *dunamis* of God by faith. Though sin has rendered us powerless in our natural state, the miraculous power of God for our salvation and moral power for a life of godliness is richly available to all sons and daughters of faith. The Bible says, *"His divine power has given us everything required for life and godliness through the knowledge of him who called us by his own glory and goodness."*[4]

The ability to break the chains of sin and live in newness of life is a daily reality of dying to the old self, picking up one's cross, and following Jesus.[5] Because the Father has declared us holy by the miraculous power of the blood and positioned us into His eternal kingdom, we have the ability to walk in the light of life. When we struggle with sin, the Holy Spirit imparts us with a sense of inner mental, spiritual, and emotional strength to have holy thoughts, attitudes, and desires.

Taking It Home

In view of the incomprehensible power of God and His working in the life of the believer, how should we think and act differently?

First, the power of God should completely transform our prayer life. Because God is omnipotent, we should have extraordinary faith. Simply put, *the church must learn to put pressure on God in prayer.* There is nothing wrong in asking God for wisdom when we pray. In fact, we should ask for wisdom,[6] but also remember that everything ultimately comes from and through God. Yes, we are called to be faithful and responsible, but God alone makes things happen. There is no better way to grow our faith than putting pressure back on God in prayer. God delights when His children trust Him completely and "pass the ball back to Him" believing He will do great and marvelous things. Remember that all things are possible with God.

Second, regardless of what this life may bring, remember that in Christ we have the *dunamis* of God to live a godly life. Though there may be seasons where we feel far from God, the Holy Spirit will never leave, and will be there to draw us back to God — the source of all our strength and hope. Scripture says, *"And we pray that you would be energized with all his explosive power from the realm of his magnificent glory, filling you with great hope."*[7]

Lastly, God's power within us extends far beyond our daily experience or limited time here on earth. In Christ, we have defeated sin and death and neither hold mastery any longer. Someday the miraculous power that rose Jesus from the dead will also raise the church from the dead. The Bible says, *"I also pray that you will understand the incredible greatness of God's power for us who believe him. This is the same mighty power that raised Christ from the dead and seated him in the place of honor at God's right hand in the heavenly realms."*[8] If the same miraculous power that rose Jesus from the dead resides within us by the Holy Spirit what in all creation — including death itself — shall prevail over God's people?

DAY 16

The Omnipotence of God

MAIN IDEA: With God all things are possible.

VERSE TO REMEMBER: *"I am the LORD God of all humanity. Nothing is too hard for me."* Jeremiah 32:27 (GW)

QUESTION TO ASK: How does my life reflect the life-changing power and presence of God?

Almighty God,

You alone possess unlimited capability and energy,

All power comes from and returns to You;

In great power the Son rose from the dead,

You defeated the last enemy,

You made all things new!

DAY 17

THE SUPREMACY OF GOD

Everything in the heavens and on earth is yours, O LORD, and this is your kingdom. We adore you as the one who is over all things.

1 CHRONICLES 29:11B (NLT)

Everything comes from him. He is the first one who was raised from the dead. So in all things Jesus has first place.

COLOSSIANS 1:18B (NCV)

God alone is on the throne.

The absolute, universal supremacy of the Almighty is positively declared in the Scriptures. There is none like Him — eternally uncreated, self-sufficient, unchangeable, unlimited in knowledge and power, universally present in all creation, holy in all His attributes, and perfect in all His ways.

The supremacy of God might be best understood by the infinite distance that separates Him from all creation — a distance not of space or time, but in the essence of His Being. Because God is transcendent, He is supreme over all. Nothing is outside His control and no plan of His can be thwarted.

When we look to Jesus Christ, we see the invisible God[1] who cannot be seen. In Christ, God's supreme rule is on display. The Bible says that through Christ all things were made, including heaven, hell, angels, the rulers and powers of this world, and all creation.[2] Nothing can be raised up over Him and nothing is beyond Him. Christ alone reigns supreme.

The Bible says, *"Heaven is my throne, and the earth is my footstool."*[3] From presidents and earthy rulers, the greatest of governments, healthiest of economies, the mightiest of men and women, most intelligent and learned, and most famous or well-known — all are but dust before the eyes of the Lord. Nations rise and nations fall, generations come, and generations go, but the Lord remains on His Holy Throne.

God's Authority, Fallen Man and the Church

Fallen man will acknowledge God in every way except as the Supreme Authority over their life. They will recognize God to be the Illustrious Maker of the universe, the Giver and Sustainer of all life, the Beacon of all the Heavens, and the King of the great seas, but when it comes to accepting God on His Holy Throne, sinful man is inclined to object. This is so because we all want authority over our life. We want to be in the control seat. Only by the grace of God through the Holy Spirit can our attitudes change so that we truly delight in God's authority over our lives.

The church sings and speaks of the supremacy of God, but does she reflect it by her actions? For many God appears to be known by the mind yet unknown by the heart. We factually accept God to be true, yet our hearts and actions often fail to reflect His Lordship over our lives. We tend to think our ways are fine, that our sins are all that bad, or that God merely looks the other way when we do wrong. Perhaps this is so because modern Christianity has produced a man-focused rather than God-focused faith, a faith that honors God with its lips but denies God with its heart.[4]

In Psalm 50, we read of God's direct confrontation with the nation of Israel. On the one hand they knew they were the chosen people of God, yet on the other hand they were living a contrary lifestyle — worshipping false gods created to look like themselves. In confronting their distorted worship, God said, *"You have done these things, and I kept silent; you thought I was just like you. But I will rebuke you and lay my case before you."*[5] If God were to directly confront the church today, would we be found to be guilty of living a contradictory lifestyle, worshipping something or someone other than the True and Living God? Would our hearts and actions match our profession of faith, reflecting the Lordship of God over our lives?

Taking It Home

We must remind our self that the church is the greatest reflection of Christ to the world. How accurately do we reflect His character? It is easier to fit into the mold of the world around us and forget to live on purpose for God. The church is called to be the light and salt of the earth and to live differently, yet there is often little variance between how the church thinks and acts from how the world thinks and acts. The church must be reminded that we will each stand before the Almighty and give an account for what we did with the precious gift of life we received — including the gift of our faith — and how we succeeded or failed in reflecting Christ to the world.

Since God alone is the absolute, supreme ruler over all things, we must live in a way that recognizes His supremacy over our life. Here are four ways we can consciously develop this kind of attitude:

First, we must acknowledge that God alone determines our path. Instead of boasting about where we will go, the things we have or do, or the business we will carry on, we must learn to think and speak in ways that acknowledge God's supremacy over our life, for nothing shall come to pass without His consent. The Bible says, *"Here's what you ought to say: 'If the Lord wills, we will live and do this or that.'"* [6]

Second, we must allow the knowledge of God supremacy to reassure our hearts. Life is not accidental nor the result of capricious chance. Your life was planned from all eternity and every facet is known by God.

Third, because God is on the throne, the world, the flesh, and the devil will not prevail over the church. Because victory over the Enemy has been decreed by God, your past has no grip, your present is secure, and your future is already provided for. The Bible affirms, "*Freedom is what we have — Christ has set us free!*[7]

The Bible guarantees that we will have troubles in life. Following Jesus will not always be easy. There will be battles, yet our lives will always be in the very capable Hands of the Father and the Son.[8] Jesus said, "*In this godless world you will continue to experience difficulties. But take heart! I've conquered the world.*" [9] Because we belong to Christ, no weapon from Satan or the demons formed against us shall prosper — ever. In fact, the very weapons the enemy once held against God's people — sin and death — have been disarmed by the cross.[10] Consequently, neither sin nor death hold mastery. This is why God's Word says we are more than a victor in Christ.[11] Because everything is under Christ's feet and spiritually-speaking we are seated next to Christ in the heavens,[12] the Enemy is under our feet as well! What assurance, what strength, what wisdom and comfort to know that we are His and that victory has already been won.

DAY 17

The Supremacy of God

MAIN IDEA: God alone is supreme and on His Holy Throne.

VERSE TO REMEMBER: "*Everything in the heavens and on earth is yours, O LORD, and this is your kingdom. We adore you as the one who is over all things.*" 1 Chronicles 29:11b (NLT)

QUESTION TO ASK: How can the knowledge of God's supremacy help me live a more victorious life in Christ?

Supreme Ruler of all,
Unlimited in knowledge and power,
Unalterable, ineffable, awesome God;
I kneel before the Holiness of Your Presence,
For You alone are worthy,
You alone are on the Throne.

DAY 18

THE SOVEREIGNTY OF GOD

My counsel shall stand, and I will accomplish all my purpose.
ISAIAH 46:10 (ESVUK)

For all things were created by him, and all things exist through him and for him. To God be the glory forever! Amen.
ROMANS 11:36 (GNT)

God is sovereign over all things.

The sovereignty of God may be understood as the *exercise* of His supremacy. Because God is supreme, He sovereignly rules over the universe. Unquestionably, the sovereignty of God is one of the most well-known and well-mentioned attributes in the Bible. The word "Lord" appears over 7,100 times in the Old Testament and is synonymous with the name of God, *Adonai*. In the New Testament, the word "Lord" appears over 600 times and is a standard title for Jesus.

Desire for Control

While we often refer to God as "Lord" in our daily vocabulary, perhaps no other attribute is more reviled by the sinful nature than the sovereignty of God.

Our proud and arrogant nature despises the fact that God alone is on the Throne and rules over everything — including the course of our life. Even the most holy and sanctified among us strive for control in some fashion or another. While we genuinely love God and others, we feel comforted knowing we can control at least part of life's outcomes. The truth is nobody controls anything. Only God determines what happens or does not happen. To willingly give up control is unnatural and rubs us all the wrong way. It forces us to place our security in God, which is sometimes easier said than done. We can work hard and make respectable plans, but we must give up control of the outcome. The Bible says, "*Within your heart you can make plans for your future, but the Lord chooses the steps you take to get there.*"[1]

God's Sovereignty and Humanity's Moral Responsibility

The theological implications of God's sovereign rule and humanity's ability to choose is challenging to understand. How can I have complete freedom of choice if God is sovereign and directs the outcome anyway? Both cannot be true, can they? The Bible teaches both realities are true — man has moral responsibility and freedom of choice, yet God is sovereign. The answer to this is simply, "yes." Answering *how* both realities work is a mystery, for human beings will never know the complete answer this side of heaven, perhaps ever.

At this point, many people object, stating that if they cannot understand a concept, they will not believe in it. Let us be careful not to make this mistake. Just because we do not understand something does not mean it is not true. Truth is not contingent upon our ability to know. Indeed, there are many things about God that our mind will never be able to grasp. Does this mean, therefore, that God ceases to be God? By no means. The Bible says, *"'My thoughts are nothing like your thoughts', says the Lord. 'And my ways are far beyond anything you could imagine. For just as the heavens are higher than the earth, so my ways are higher than your ways and my thoughts than your thoughts.'"* [2]

Be that as it may, there are helpful ways to understand this paradox. As an example: In God's sovereignty, He decreed that man should have *limited freedom to choose*. Man cannot have *absolute freedom* because we are not God and not wholly independent. We do, however, have the freedom to make decisions within our human capability because God declared it so. If we choose evil God's sovereignty is not countered but fulfilled. If we choose good God's sovereignty is not countered but fulfilled. Either way, whether we choose good or evil, God is still sovereign and on His throne. In other words, if in God's absolute freedom, He sovereignly decreed that man should have the ability to choose, why should anyone object? The only reason we have this ability is because God is sovereign.

To clarify this point further, let's use an analogy: A father and his son are standing in the driveway and the father is holding his son's hand. The father knows that if he lets go of his son's hand he will run into the street. The father lets go of his son's hand. His son runs into the street. Whose will was it for the son to run into the street? The son's or the father's?

Taking It Home

Relationships or situations may be incredibly unfair or difficult at times. The trials of life can be overwhelming, and we often wonder whether the wrongs will ever be made right. God knows every careless word, every evil action, and every motive of the heart. He knows our situations and every unfair circumstance. Regardless of what each day brings God's will is that we turn from sin, do the right thing, and trust His sovereignty to work the rest out.

Because God desires to see us grow His actions toward us are intentional. Expect moments where people, situations, or opportunities will cross your path that serve a higher, divine purpose. Some of these encounters or events will be exciting while others will force you to step out of your comfort entirely. Still others may appear to be a complete inconvenience at best. Some may appear to very ordinary or routine. Either way remember that moment-by-moment God is intentionally at work in your life.

Bottom line: when all is said and done, we should live our life in view of the true life to come. This life will go by in a blink of an eye. In Christ, we have hope of eternal life and victory over daily sin and our eventual death. Whether or not people choose to place their faith in Jesus Christ, someday every nation, tribe, people, and language will kneel before the Son of God and acknowledge His sovereign authority, for He alone is worthy of all worship.

DAY 18

The Sovereignty of God

MAIN IDEA: Because God is sovereign, I can know He is in control.

VERSE TO REMEMBER: *"For all things were created by him, and all things exist through him and for him. To God be the glory forever! Amen."* Romans 11:36 (GNT)

QUESTION TO ASK: In view of God's sovereignty, what parts of my life do I need to trust Him better?

Lord of history, King of all things,
Nothing is too great,
None too difficult for You;
You direct the course of my life,
And guide my every step,
In You do I trust.

DAY 19

THE VERACITY OF GOD

God is light; in him there is no darkness at all.
1 JOHN 1:5B (NIV)

Your Word is truth! So make them holy by the truth.
JOHN 17:17 (TPT)

Truth finds its origin in God, its incarnation in Christ, and present manifestation in the written Word of God, the Bible.[1]

There never has been a time, nor will be a time, when God is not impeccably true. Because God is true, He cannot lie. Because God is true, no attribute or divine act of His can ever be false. God is the source of all truth. Since God exists in resplendent, unapproachable light, truth can only be known once it is first given. Jesus' mission was to bring this light of God's truth to the world. When Jesus spoke, He spoke words given Him from the Father.[2] Because He and the Father are one, Jesus is, therefore, the very truth of God in bodily form.

Throughout His three-and-a-half-year ministry, Jesus' teaching centered around the truth: The Father in Heaven is the true God. The kingdom of God is based on truth. Jesus words and actions are done in truth, and those who believe upon Him are children of the truth.

The inspired, written Word is the infallible truth of God given to mankind. It is a guiding light unto our path,[3] spiritual food for our soul,[4] and the god-breathed authority for Christian practice.[5] Because God's Word is eternal[6] it can never be reversed, removed, or negated.

General Revelation

For thousands of years, humankind has inquired into the building blocks of reality. The more we learn, the more we realize how much we do not know. What man calls "laws of nature" are in fact the intelligent framework of God upheld by the truthfulness of His spoken Word. Laws of quantum physics, classical mechanics, gravitation and relativity, electromagnetism, and photonics are all testaments to the exact precision of His nature. The Bible says, "*The heavens declare the glory of God, and the sky displays what his hands have made.*"[7] Truly, the universe and all creation testify to the veracity of God.

While every human being knows there is an Intelligent Creator and can observe certain truths about God through creation and science, general knowledge is insufficient to save. Only through the particular revelation of God; namely, Jesus Christ and the written Word, can man come to the saving knowledge of God.

Particular Revelation

Because of sin we are incapable of knowing and understanding God in our natural state. God must do a supernatural work in our mind and heart by the Spirit to shine truth into the dark corners of our heart.

To use an example:

We are like the flawlessly designed automobile that was seized and compacted from several directions. While we still can tell it is an automobile, it is nothing like the original design. In the same manner, sin has seized humanity and our mental, spiritual, and emotional life is a shadow of what we were designed by God to be. As the compacted automobile is incapable of operating, so too our natural faculties are incapable of understanding and loving God. Only through the transformative light of Jesus Christ can we come to a saving knowledge of God. Scripture reveals, *"The God who said, "Out of darkness the light shall shine!" is the same God who made his light shine in our hearts, to bring us the knowledge of God's glory shining in the face of Christ."* [8]

Jesus Christ, the *Logos* of God

Ancient Greek philosophy centered around answering the ultimate questions of reality. They wanted to know what truth was and the ultimate reality behind everything we see and observe. To the Greeks, whatever was behind everything is ultimate truth. The term they came up with to describe this ultimate reality was *logos.*

In the first chapter of the Gospel of John, the apostle marries this ancient question with the incarnation of Jesus Christ, "*In the beginning was the Word, and the Word was with God, and the Word was God,*"[9] followed by "*the Word became flesh and made his dwelling among us.*"[10] The term used for "word" in both verses is *logos.*

To the Greeks, John's statement would have been an unfathomable concept to consider since they believed physical to be evil and spiritual to be good. The spiritual or ultimate truth itself taking on the physical was simply unheard of. Moreover, unlike the Greeks who believed that the *logos* was an impersonal force, the apostle made it abundantly clear that ultimate truth — Jesus Christ — is not an impersonal force but very personal God that desires relationship with humanity.

The *Logos* and the Shadow of Death

As followers of the Lord Jesus this life is a pilgrimage toward the Holy City of God, the New Jerusalem.[11] Since we are strangers merely passing through, this world will cast a myriad of distractions, hurdles, and attacks our way in attempt to steer us off the straight and narrow. We must not be unaware of this. Our battle is not against people but against the unseen spiritual forces of evil. These dark forces, otherwise known as the spirits of fear, doubt, anxiety, lust, greed, and deception (to name a few) want to destroy our faith and keep us from God. While this is a somber thought to consider, it is a healthy and necessary meditation. We are to be as wise as serpents and as innocent as doves.[12]

The *Logos* of God, the written Word of God, and the Holy Spirit are our weapons of righteousness. Let us remember that God is a personal God and that Jesus is on the journey with us. The Bible says, "*...I will never leave you or abandon you.*"[13] The Word of God is truth for the soul and a light unto our path. As our Divine Counselor the Holy Spirit will be there to strengthen our inner spirit, equipping our minds for battle.

Taking It Home

In view of the truthfulness of God's very character and nature, how should we respond in a way that brings glory to His Name?

First, the veracity of God is not just a scientific observation, it is a life-changing message that is experienced daily throughout the world. No other gospel changes lives like the message of Jesus crucified and risen from the dead. Because saving faith is only possible through hearing the Word of God it must be proclaimed.[14] When God's Word is spoken, truth is being declared into the spiritual realm and carries tremendous power.

Second, remember that as a Christian, this world is not our home. Our citizenship is in heaven. Since our lifelong battle is not against flesh and blood but the spiritual forces of evil, we must be on guard. Let us not be unaware of the enemy's schemes that want to trip up our walk with God. The best way to deny evil forces is to spend time equipping our minds with truth — the Word of God.

Finally, some glorious day, there shall be no more night, no more darkness, and no more evil. When God establishes the New Jerusalem, the city of God, the sons and daughters of the light will dwell in God's holy presence. The old order of things will have passed away and the truthfulness of God shall prevail. God Himself will be the eternal light of His people and we shall reign for ever and ever.

DAY 19

The Veracity of God

MAIN IDEA: God is perfectly true in every way.

VERSE TO REMEMBER: *"God is light; in him there is no darkness at all."* 1 John 1:5b (NIV)

QUESTION TO ASK: How does the truthfulness of God give me strength and bright hope?

Everlasting God,
You are infinitely true;
The foundations of reality are found in You,
For Your Word is perfect and final,
And Your light is my life,
My bright hope.

DAY 20

THE WRATH OF GOD

For God in heaven unveils his holy anger breaking forth against every form of sin, both toward ungodliness that lives in hearts and evil actions.
ROMANS 1:18A (TPT)

The one who believes in the Son has eternal life, but the one who rejects the Son will not see life; instead, the wrath of God remains on him.
JOHN 3:36 (CSB)

God's wrath is His infinite love and justice in action against sin.

For many, the wrath of God is a challenging attribute to consider. At one time or another, all of us have wrestled with questions such as:

> *"If God is all-loving, isn't it contradictory for God to also show wrath?"*
>
> *"If God keeps record for the coming day of accountability, isn't that a cruel and unloving thing to do?"*

> *"If God condemns sinners to eternal punishment, isn't that unfair and unjust? After all, only God is perfect."*
>
> *"If God is all-powerful, why can't He simply forgive and forget?"*

These questions are very real. Sadly, they are also questions many never find (or want) answers to. For some, they are questions that keep them from accepting God. The truth is, when God's wrath is properly understood it does not contradict his nature, rather it fulfills it. Let us look at three foundational reason that bring this all-important and necessary attribute together:

> First, *God alone determines what is right and wrong.*
>
> Second, *God is just.*
>
> Third, *God is love.*

God Alone is Determines What is Right and Wrong

"In a perfect Garden long ago, humankind made a choice. The serpent had slithered into the lives of Adam and Eve and his indictment against God was that God was a liar. The plot was set. Satan's trap was to tempt the man and his wife to partake of the fruit of the tree of the knowledge of good and evil, and the bait the serpent used was "wisdom." Satan knew that when they partook of the fruit their eyes would be opened and they would be like God, becoming gods." [1] Then, for the first time, the man and woman could determine — in their own mind — what was right or wrong. No longer would they be guided under God's rule but instead by the compass of their own mind.

Humanity has not changed since. The sinful mind naturally repels us from God's truth. It places one's own mental compass and even life experience above the truth of God's Word. If a concept does not make sense or life experience beats you down, like the serpent, the sinful nature will always be there to slither its way between you and God. We must be mindful that the enemy is relentless — particularly in telling us something is good when it only poses as such, or bad when it is truly good. God's Word is a gift to humanity. It is our guiding light. It reveals not only the condition of our hearts and our need for God, but what His character and nature are like. God alone is the very standard that weighs what is right and wrong, good or bad.

God is Just

Because God just, He rules the universe based on the standard of His holiness. Since God is holy, He is the very standard and definition of moral goodness. Now, if God is good and judges the world impartially, we would not call God holy and good if He turned the other way when we sinned or acted unjustly. In the same way we would not call an earthly judge good if he forgave a wrongdoer because the judge had pity. We would call this judge bad because he is not bringing justice.

If our expectation for earthly judges is to maintain justice on earth, how much more ought we to expect the Creator to maintain justice in everything? The truth is, whenever we sin someone must pay for it — either we pay or someone else pays. If a child broke a lamp, either the child will have to pay or the parent. The lamp will not suddenly replace itself.

God is Love

Because God is love, His pursuit of your heart is so relentless that He was willing to sacrifice His own son so that your sins may be forgiven. Think about that...even though your sin once stood in opposition to His holiness, God's holy hatred for sin was satisfied through the justice of the cross. This was God's plan for you from the very beginning. Before you came into bring, you were already loved. The Bible says, *"This is real love — not that we loved God, but that he loved us and sent his Son as a sacrifice to take away our sins."*[2] Through Jesus' blood God's holy wrath for our sin was paid in full!

Jewish Passover, a Prophecy Fulfilled

Though the cross was God's plan of salvation from the very beginning, the love and justice of God for our salvation was foreshadowed many years before the birth of the Savior. In the Old Testament we read the Lord's declaration that his servant Moses would lead the Hebrew people out of slavery in Egypt. To free them from bondage, God instructed Moses that the eighth and final plague over the land would be the plague of death. To avoid God's swift and coming judgement, God instructed Moses to tell the Hebrew people to slaughter a lamb that was without stain or spot and to cover the entrance of their homes with the blood. When the coming judgment of death swept over the land, God promised that death would pass over every home whose entrance was covered with the blood of the lamb. Instead of experiencing judgment, they would be liberated from bondage and set free.[3]

1,500 years after this event Jesus came into the world to forgive sins — once and for all. Like the Hebrew people who were held in bondage to the Egyptians, the Bible says that all humanity is held in bondage to sin and are helpless to liberate ourselves. Because God is just, sin cannot be overlooked, but because God is love the Father sent His only begotten Son — the perfect, sinless Lamb — to satisfy the punishment we justly deserved. God did this so we could be set free from our bondage to sin. The amazing thing is that Jesus' crucifixion was during Passover, the annual Jewish holiday to commemorate the day in which death and judgment passed over the homes of the Hebrew people in Egypt. Because Jesus is the Lamb of God whose blood was shed for the world, we have been liberated from the power of sin and coming judgement. When the Day of God's wrath comes, eternal punishment for sin shall pass over the sons and daughters of God *if the blood of His Son covers the entrance of our heart.* The Bible says, "*You were bought with the precious blood of Christ's death. He was a pure and perfect sacrificial Lamb.*"[4]

Taking It Home

While God's wrath may appear to be confusing or even contradictory, it is a very necessary part of reality and of the gospel. Because God is just, we can know that He will always act according to the standard of His moral goodness, but because God is love, we can know that death and eternal judgment for sin has been satisfied through Jesus Christ! Amen!

DAY 20

The Wrath of God

MAIN IDEA: God's holy wrath toward sin was satisfied in Jesus Christ.

VERSE TO REMEMBER: "*The one who believes in the Son has eternal life, but the one who rejects the Son will not see life; instead, the wrath of God remains on him.*" John 3:36 (CSB)

QUESTION TO ASK: Have I trusted in the precious blood of Jesus Christ to forgive me for all my sin?

O Holy God,
Before Your presence who can stand?
Your Holiness is a consuming fire,
Yet in infinite love, You did satisfy,
Eternal wrath, Thy justice due.

DAY 21

THE MYSTERY OF GOD

We speak of God's hidden and mysterious wisdom that God decided to use for our glory long before the world began.
1 CORINTHIANS 2:7 (CEV)

Listen, and I will tell you a divine mystery: not all of us will die, but we will all be transformed. It will happen in an instant — in the twinkling of his eye.
1 CORINTHIANS 15:51-52A (TPT)

GOD IS A GOD OF HIDDEN AND UNVEILED MYSTERIES.

The mystery of God is an attribute not just because God is incomprehensible, but by virtue of His very essence. The Bible says that the hidden things belong to the Lord[1] and truth is only known once it is first given. While God has chosen to reveal certain truths about Himself, namely, His attributes, the complete knowledge of God and His plans will forever remain a mystery. Who among us has never stopped and wondered, "What lies outside the universe?" or "What will we do in heaven for all eternity?" The answer to questions such as these may forever remain a mystery, hidden in God Himself.

The Veiled Mystery

When one observes the full counsel of Scripture, it become apparent that revelation did not come from God to humanity at once, but in stages. In His infinite wisdom, God did not reveal everything to Abraham, Moses, and David, or even the prophets, but sovereignly choose to reveal certain truths to different people at different times. Though the revelation they received was veiled in mystery, they maintained forward-looking faith in God.

The apostle Peter, in speaking of the veiled mystery the prophets and forefathers received, said the they searched deeply about the gift of life that God was preparing and of the Messiah that was to come. While they did know the Messiah must suffer and then be followed by glory, they did not know *who* this Messiah would be or *when* these things would come to pass. Moreover, they did not realize that the Messiah would come in two stages — the first time as a gentle Lamb[2] and the second time as a conquering Lion.[3] Even Jesus' own disciples were unable to recognize the full extent of His mission until the Lord rose from the dead and the Holy Spirit came upon them!

The Unveiled Mystery

While the church now has the complete answer to which the prophets and forefathers of old searched so intently to know — the gospel of Jesus Christ — we, too, are still left in mystery, though of a different sort. Although our faith looks back to the cross and sees the fulfillment of God's plan for salvation, our hope looks forward to the ultimate fulfillment of it. While the Word of God does reveal truth about Jesus' final return, much remains a mystery. We do not know when Jesus will return, nor do we know everything about the wonderous resurrection of the dead. These are glories yet to be...

All who are in Christ, including those who have already passed on, have yet to experience the greatest climax of human history — the very reason why Jesus came to earth — to bring life and immortality. The certainty that we shall all rise from death to eternal life is a prophecy yet to be fulfilled for all who are in Christ. The Bible says, "*Listen to this secret truth: we shall not all die, but when the last trumpet sounds, we shall all be changed in an instant, as quickly as the blinking of an eye. For when the trumpet sounds, the dead will be raised, never to die again, and we shall all be changed.*"[4]

The astounding fact is the Christian faith hangs its very own validity on one single thread. A thread that, if severed, would cause the entire counsel of God's Word to fall apart — and that thread is the resurrection. The Bible maintains, "*For if there is no such thing as a resurrection from the dead, then not even Christ has been raised. And if Christ has not been raised, all of our preaching has been for nothing and your faith is useless.*"[5]

Regarding the historical value of the gospel and how a mysterious "something" must have occurred, philosopher and leading scholar on the resurrection William Lane Craig writes: "It is quite clear that without the belief in the resurrection the Christian faith could not have come into being. The disciples would have remained crushed and defeated men. Even had they continued to remember Jesus as their believed teacher, His crucifixion would have forever silenced any hopes of His being the Messiah. The cross would have remained the sad and shameful end to His career. *The origin of Christianity therefore hinges on the belief of the early disciples that God had raised Jesus from the dead.*"[6]

Because Jesus indeed rose from the dead, we are not without hope. For if the first witnesses had an extraordinary, blessed faith, how much more blessed shall we be? Jesus said, *"Thomas, do you have faith because you have seen me? The people who have faith in me without seeing me are the ones who are really blessed!"*[7]

Let us rejoice that our faith unifies us in Jesus' death in order that we shall be unified in His resurrection.[8] This is the gospel that we cling to and hold so dearly: *Jesus Christ, the Creator and Sustainer, The Son of God, The Son of Man, The Word that became flesh, Immanuel, The Holy One of God,* and *The Way, The Truth, and the Life* was crucified in weakness but was raised in power. He died in dishonor yet was raised in honor. He was spat on, mocked, beaten, and nailed to the tree; yet He was raised in splendor, power, authority, and everlasting glory. Jesus Christ *is* the *King of kings* and the *Lord of lords* who triumphed over sin and death by His glorious resurrection. Hallelujah!

Taking It Home

The death and resurrection of Christ is good news to a dying world! While our own resurrection is ultimately a prophecy yet to be fulfilled, its revelation has been unveiled for all to see. Though God needs none to accomplish His divine purposes, He chooses to use His people, the church, as His primary instrument to carry the gospel to the nations. We must not keep the marvelous gift of Jesus' death and resurrection to our self. The gift was meant for the world.

DAY 21

The Mystery of God

MAIN IDEA: Though God is in many ways mysterious, He has revealed to the world His plan of salvation.

VERSE TO REMEMBER: *"Listen, and I will tell you a divine mystery: not all of us will die, but we will all be transformed. It will happen in an instant—in the twinkling of his eye."* 1 Corinthians 15:51-52a (TPT)

QUESTION TO ASK: Does the promise of the future resurrection give me great hope and good cheer?

God of mystery,
In obscurity You dwell,
Yet by love, God with us, Immanuel;
Revealed to the humble heart,
By the Spirit, mystery unveiled,
Everlasting life,
Freedom prevailed.

THE GOODNESS OF GOD

DAY 22

THE GOODNESS OF GOD

All generous giving and every perfect gift is from above, coming down from the Father of lights, with whom there is no variation or the slightest hint of change.
JAMES 1:17A (NET BIBLE)

You are good and do good; teach me your statutes.
PSALM 119:68 (ESV)

Because God is great, He is greatly to be feared. Because God is both Great and Good, He can be *trusted*, *known*, and *loved*.

The goodness of God is not the same as the Holiness of God which is His separate, distinct nature. God's goodness is that which leads Him to be benevolent and compassionate toward creation. The moral attributes of grace, mercy, faithfulness, justice, and the multifaceted characteristics that are identified as His love demonstrate God's goodness in action.

Holy Scripture reveals the goodness of God in two over-all ways. The first is the general goodness God bestows upon all creation. The second is the particular goodness God demonstrates in relationship through Jesus Christ.

God's General Goodness

Because God is good, He cares for creation in a variety of natural ways, including sunshine, rain, and sustenance. This type of goodness God bestows upon all humanity, including those who do right and those who do wrong. The Bible says, "*He makes the sun rise on both good and bad people. And he sends rain for the ones who do right and for the ones who do wrong.*"[1]

While the goodness of God upon those who do evil is temporal in nature and confined strictly to this life, the goodness of God for those who are in Christ is eternal and extends beyond this life.

God's Particular Goodness

The particular goodness of God is most eminently demonstrated in the person and work of Jesus Christ, through whom we learn how God relates to people.

In the gospels, we see how Jesus responded to different people. To those who are hard-hearted and stubborn, they will find Jesus to be cold, aloof, and offensive. Yet to the humble, tender heart that sincerely seeks Him, they will find Jesus to be gentle, kind, compassionate, and overflowing with grace and mercy. Whether Christians realize it or not, we also reflect the aroma of God's essence. The Bible says, *"It is the fragrance of Christ within us, an aroma to both the saved and the unsaved all around us. To those who are not being saved, we seem a fearful smell of death and doom, while to those who know Christ we are a life-giving perfume"*[2]

God's Goodness Upon His Children

When one shows sincerity in wanting to be reconciled to God and eagerness to be forgiven, their desire is often combined with hesitancy because the burden of past sins. The conscience weighs heavy since one recognizes they've broken God's moral standard, and their heart desires to be freed of this guilt. Approaching the cross for the first time is humbling. One wonders, "If I kneel before the Savior, what will He be like and How will He act toward me?" The answer is found in the goodness of God.

In Christ, the abundant goodness of God cascades down from the Father of Lights. When we feel overwhelmed and ready to give up, we find rest. When we have suffered tremendous loss, we receive comfort. When we seek God above all our hearts will be full. When we show care for others, we discover the kindness of God. When we draw near to His presence, we begin to see God in the world around us. When we help resolve conflict or care for the need of another, we experience the peace of God. When we are insulted, mocked, or misunderstood because of God we will only want to live for God more. In all things we shall be blessed. The Scriptures teach that the fruit of these all-encompassing truths are born when we stick close to God, *"...blessed is the man who trusts me, God, the woman who sticks with God. They're like trees replanted in Eden, putting down roots near the rivers — never a worry through the hottest of summers, never dropping a leaf, serene and calm through droughts, bearing fresh fruit every season."* [3]

Taking It Home

The goodness of God provides the Christian security and encouragement. It draws us to Him and reminds us that God has good purposes and intentions for our life. Because God is unchanging, we can know that His goodness toward us will never change.

By walking in relationship with the Heavenly Father we not only experience the richness of His goodness but are called to reciprocate the same goodness in relationship with others. God's Word says, "*But the fruit produced by the Holy Spirit within you is divine love in all its varied expressions: joy that overflows, peace that subdues, patience that endures, kindness in action, a life full of virtue, faith that prevails, gentleness of heart, and strength of spirit. Never set the law above these qualities, for they are meant to be limitless.*"[4]

Experiencing God's goodness and reciprocating in relationship with others is not automatic. The sinful nature is at war with the Spirit of God. Both stand in opposition to one another. Living in the sinful nature is easier than walking in the Spirit. Because this is so we must learn to crucify and starve our sinful nature each day and choose to live in the Spirit. We must learn to feed and enrich our souls with God's presence and the life-giving Word, for it is possible to have the Spirit and the Word but not walk in them. We must acquire the habit of responding in ways that honor God and promote the good of others.

In and through all these things God's power and unlimited capability in our lives is a reservoir which awaits.

DAY 22

The Goodness of God

MAIN IDEA: Because God is good, He can be trusted, known, and loved.

VERSE TO REMEMBER: *"All generous giving and every perfect gift is from above, coming down from the Father of lights, with whom there is no variation or the slightest hint of change."* James 1:17a (NET Bible)

QUESTION TO ASK: How does my life reflect the goodness of God?

You alone, O God, are Good,
For from Your Hand comes every good thing;
In You do I have life, and through You I am sustained;
May I learn to be like You, reflecting Your goodness.

DAY 23

THE KINDNESS OF GOD

Yes, I have loved you with an everlasting love; Therefore with lovingkindness I have drawn you.
JEREMIAH 31:3 (NKJV)

How excellent is Your lovingkindness, O God! Therefore mankind seeks refuge in the shadow of Your wings.
PSALM 36:7 (MEV)

THE LOVINGKINDNESS OF GOD IS EVERLASTING.

When we say that God is kind, we do not mean the same type of kindness human beings often show to one another such as a pleasant smile or seeking to get along without "ruffling someone's feathers." God's kindness is qualitatively different. It is His generous patience and care, intended to lead us toward a better place with Him, and flows out of His everlasting love for mankind.

In His wisdom and providence, God knows exactly what it takes to stir our heart and draw us to Him. Sometimes God intervenes. Other times God will allow events to occur. Either way, God knows what is most suitable toward forming godliness in our life, particularly through repentance. The Bible says, *"Do you realize that all the wealth of his extravagant kindness is meant to melt your heart and lead you into repentance?"*[1] When the heart responds positively to God, refreshment and blessing from His presence always follow.[2]

Encountering God

Everyone desires a pleasant life, yet life in Christ will not always be so. Pain, hurt, and loss are inevitable and often cuts deep into the fabric of our soul. In those moments or seasons, it is easy to doubt God's goodness and even accuse His integrity. Questioning follows as the heart decries:

> *"Why would You allow me to go through this?"*
>
> *"I've been faithful to follow You and now I am hurting... why, O God?"*
>
> *"What are You doing? Everything was just fine!"*

In those moments and seasons, it is easy to miss the goodness of God and give rise to anger, resentment, and fear. It isn't easy to look above the pain, past the hurt, and beyond the loss and see the bigger picture. Difficulty, pain, and struggle naturally tends to narrow our perspective, not widen it; to contract, not expand our soul.

The Bible says that God has good intentions toward you.[3] Because this is infinitely true, there will be times you will just have to trust that God knows what He is doing. Like God's providence, His kindness is often most recognizable in hindsight. We look back and see how God used the experiences we encountered so that we might encounter Him. When this realization happens, a sigh of relief streams across the landscape of your heart, the floodgates of grace wash over your soul, and inner peace is restored. Often when the morning dawn breaks the night, when healing emerges from the pain, and when clarity aerates from the confusion do we then marvel, "Oh me of little faith! Why did I ever distrust the Lord my God?"

This is why it can be said of the Proverbs 31 woman, *"Strength and honor are her clothing, and she can laugh at the time to come."*[4] A woman or man of God knows that God's love is everlasting, and His kindness will never cease. When difficulties emerge, or consequences for our or other's actions ensue, God's kindness does not evaporate but will always be there, falling fresh upon you to envelope you in His grace; even if you are unable to perceive it in the moment.

Taking It Home

Though God's kindness is qualitatively different than the casual sort of kindness human beings tends to display, the kindness of God's people is also markedly different. The Bible says that kindness is a fruit of the Spirit,[5] a mark of a Christian, and flows out of a good heart with good intentions for another. Whether it be sacrificial giving of material possessions or time, edifying words to build up another, patience or care in a situation that requires delicacy, wisely correcting someone who is in error, or reassuring counsel in times of uncertainty. All are acts of kindness where generosity, thoughtfulness, patience, and care are used. Like the other fruits of the Spirit, when showing kindness, we should not let our left hand know what our right hand is doing.[6] Kindness works best when it flows out of who you are in Christ. Just the same, we must be careful to examine our hearts so that our actions are not done for the praise of men but for God.[7]

The kindness of God is inherent to the gospel. In fact, the gospel epitomizes the kindness of God. Let us for a moment try and step away from our human perspective and look at things objectively. Since God is holy and righteous, is not God justified to condemn sin and evil? Are not we guilty of rebellion against His moral standard of goodness? Instead of God giving humanity what we rightly deserve — condemnation, God, in His everlasting love, has demonstrated tremendous restraint through the cross. The fact that we even have an option to accept or not accept Christ is a testimony to God's generous patience and care. The Bible says, *"Don't you see how wonderfully kind, tolerant, and patient God is with you? Does this mean nothing to you? Can't you see that his kindness is intended to turn you from your sin?"* [8]

Moreover, not only has God demonstrated His kindness through the one act of the cross, but God goes above and beyond this one act of love through passionately pursuing us in a thousand different ways each day. Like the church of Laodicea, God stands at the door of our hearts knocking.[9] He awaits the daily invitation to dine at the table of our heart. He will not demand we invite Him in. He must be invited. Truly, God is a gentleman.

DAY 23

The Kindness of God

MAIN IDEA: God's kindness is His generous patience and care, intended to lead me to a better place with Him.

VERSE TO REMEMBER: *"Yes, I have loved you with an everlasting love; Therefore with lovingkindness I have drawn you."* Jeremiah 31:3 (NKJV)

QUESTION TO ASK: How do I see God's kindness at work in my life?

O God, gratitude can never express,
Your generous patience, abounding care,
And everlasting compassion;
You pursue me each day anew,
Stirring my heart back to You.

DAY 24

THE GRACE OF GOD

For the grace of God has appeared that offers salvation to all people.
TITUS 2:11 (NIV)

God saved you by his grace when you believed. And you can't take credit for this; it is a gift from God. Salvation is not a reward for the good things we have done, so none of us can boast about it.
EPHESIANS 2:8-9 (NLT)

GRACE CANNOT BE EARNED, IT MUST BE GIVEN.

From all eternity, the grace of God has always been associated with Jesus Christ. God is a God of grace, and no one was ever saved apart from grace. In the days prior to Jesus, men and women of God demonstrated forward-looking faith as they trusted God's Word and eagerly awaited the Messiah. For the church today, our faith looks back to Calvary and the finished work of Christ. The eternal grace of God was always at the center.

From Adam and Eve to the present day, humanity has always needed God's grace. Our sheer dependency encompasses more than just our existence. It includes our need of salvation and daily forgiveness. While technological and scientific developments have made great progress over the millennia, our dependency on grace remains the same. Humanity can send human beings to outer space, transplant the human heart, and cure diseases, yet we cannot reach God's heaven, transform our sinful condition, or cure the disease of sin.

Because sin cannot be cured and is inherent,[1] there is nothing we can do to stop sin from being passed down to the next generation. No toddler needed to be trained to scream the word "mine!" or to throw a tantrum when they do not get their way. Though humans grow into adulthood, we never outgrow sin. Our selfish pride just takes on a more sophisticated, deceitful form. The Bible says, *"The human mind is the most deceitful of all things. It is incurable. No one can understand how deceitful it is."*[2] Only God's grace can cure the disease of sin, transform our sinful condition, and make us right before Him.

Debt Erased and Merit Credited

Because all humanity has sinned and fallen short of God's perfect standard of holiness[3] each of us carry the debt of condemnation because of our sin.[4] In God's goodness, however, His grace imputes merit even though we've missed the mark and declares our debt to be canceled even though we owe it. In other words, the grace of God is His goodness applied toward our demerit and debt. The Bible says, *"He erased it all — our sins, our stained soul — he deleted it all and they cannot be retrieved! Everything we once were in Adam has been placed onto his cross and nailed permanently there as a public display of cancellation."*[5]

No amount of good works could ever earn, achieve, receive, or merit God's grace. His grace is an undeserved gift. Salvation was never based on how good one is or attempts to be. One can get baptized, pray each day, memorize verses, and care for the poor, but these valiant efforts will not save. Trusting in one's own efforts and even sincere Christian obedience is an offense to a holy and perfect God. It is an offense because it places trust and merit in self rather than trust and merit in God. Only God is meritorious. The Bible says, "*We're all sin-infected, sin-contaminated. Our best efforts are grease- stained rags.*" [6]

The Internal Battle

Since the days of Adam, a cosmic war between the forces of good and the forces of evil has been plain to see. What is less plain to see is that the daily battle ground takes place in our own mind. Our thoughts steer the entire course of our life. As long as we are in the body and on this earth, we will always be fighting this battle. The mind of fallen man cannot be trusted. It does not mean that we are incapable of moral, upright decisions and thoughts. We are quite capable of thinking and doing much good, but this is only so because of the infinite goodness of God. What it does mean, however, is that the sinful mind is predisposed toward pride and selfishness — the two deadly vices at the root of sin and are especially difficult to detect. We are so used to hearing our own thoughts that we trick ourselves into believing we are morally and spiritually better off than we are. The Bible says, "*You may think everything you do is right, but the LORD judges your motives.*"[7]

Because we dwell within our own thoughts, we need the outside infusion of God's truth to recalibrate our thoughts and attitudes. This infusion comes by grace through the power of the Holy Spirit, providing the ability to walk in a manner that pleases God. Another way to say it would be that the grace of

God meets us just as we are and draws us closer to becoming the person God intends us to be. Grace renews the soul, cleanses the conscience, enlightens the mind, fortifies the inner being, cheers the heart, and purifies and elevates one's thoughts. In short, grace enables us to be the best version of our self.

Extending Grace to One Another

Morning by morning as you live by grace, remember that God desires others to come to know His grace as well. The Bible says, "*Watch over each other to make sure that no one misses the revelation of God's grace. And make sure no one lives with a root of bitterness sprouting within them which will only cause trouble and poison the hearts of many.*"[8] As the body of Christ, we are responsible for one another. We all fall short, whether knowingly or unknowingly and need grace and forgiveness. One of the distinguishing marks of those who know Jesus is the ability to forgive and extend grace to another. It is the way of God and is to be the way of the Christian. Failing to extend forgiveness and grace not only potentially harms the one in need of forgiveness, but always harms the one who needs to forgive.

In the Gospel of Matthew, we read a parable Jesus taught about a king who wanted to settle accounts with his servants. After finding out how much each servant owed him, the king decided to cancel all their debts. One of the king's servants (whose canceled debt amounted to 10,000 bags of gold, or 200,000 years' worth of a day labor's wages) went out to one of his fellow servants who in turn owed him 100 silver coins, or the average daily wage. Instead of canceling his fellow servant's debt like the king had done for him, he had this fellow servant thrown into prison until he could repay the debt in full. When the king learned of this he was outraged and exclaimed, "*You scoundrel! Is this the way you respond to my mercy? Because you begged me, I forgave you the massive debt that you owed me. Why didn't you show the same mercy to your fellow servant that I showed to you?"*[9] In fury the king had this servant thrown into prison until he should repay all of his debt — a debt so astronomically large it would have been impossible for this one man to ever repay. Jesus concluded that this is how the Heavenly Father will also treat us if we do not forgive a brother or sister from the heart. Clearly, extending grace and forgiveness is pivotal to God and carries eternal significance.

Taking It Home

Because we have received the gift of grace, we are now free to extend grace to perhaps the most difficult person in our lives to extend grace to - our own self. There are two sides here. Some struggle with treating our self so poorly that it leads to self- condemnation. This is a form of pride that exalts self over God by refusing to receive His grace at all. Others struggle with repudiating God's grace because we would rather earn merit through our own efforts. This is a form of self-centeredness in order to feel worthy of Him. Neither are of God. Both are sin and oppose the gospel of Jesus Christ. Let us not be deceived, for the Enemy works in subtle, clever ways, including self-denigrating pride that allows us to show extravagant grace to another but cheap grace toward self, or impossible merit through one's effort. While both may appear to be humble on the outside, it remains far from God's grace on the inside.

There is always fine line with grace. We must not take advantage of it and have no remorse for our sin. Yet we must also readily accept grace joyfully. The Holy Spirit's job is to help us find the right heart balance. We can be remorseful for sin yet accepting of grace synchronously. God's grace is sufficient for every circumstance.

While the Bible makes it clear that we are to do good works, the good works themselves do not save. They only validate that our faith in Christ is authentic. Put another way, we do not do good works to be saved but because we already are saved. A life filled with good works always flows out of a heart that has come to know the incomparable grace of God.

Forgiveness is one of the most powerful forces in the universe. It sets one free to be the best version of themselves. It brings health to the mind, spirit, emotions, and physical body. It loosens the ties of sin and expels the Enemy from our life. It softens the heart of another. It demonstrates the love of God and brings Him glory. Freedom always flows from forgiveness.

DAY 24

The Grace of God

MAIN IDEA: God's grace is sufficient in every detail of my life.

VERSE TO REMEMBER: *God saved you by his grace when you believed. And you can't take credit for this; it is a gift from God. Salvation is not a reward for the good things we have done, so none of us can boast about it."* Ephesians 2:8-9 (NLT)

QUESTION TO ASK: Do I tend to lean on my own "goodness" to be accepted by God, or do I find rest in His grace alone?

Sweet, amazing grace,
On the cross, You took my place;
My debt canceled, my punishment absolved,
Righteousness by faith, God resolved;
Grace, grace, amazing grace,
On the cross, You took my place.

DAY 25

THE MERCY OF GOD

Return to the LORD your God, for he is merciful and compassionate, slow to get angry and filled with unfailing love.
JOEL 2:13B (NLT)

So let us come boldly to the very throne of God and stay there to receive his mercy and to find grace to help us in our times of need.
HEBREWS 4:16 (TLB)

INFINITE MERCIES STREAM FROM HIS PRESENCE.

Contrary to popularized notions of rulers whose monarchy is defined by autocracy or tyranny, the rule of God over the universe is defined by His Holiness. Because God is holy and good, we may find mercy and grace before His throne in our time of need.[1] Access to the Father is available through the blood of Jesus Christ which cleanses and purifies us from all sin. In Christ, we now have confidence to approach our Father who knows our plight of sin, that we live in a broken world, and the repercussions thereof.

God's Tender Mercies

The word for mercy in the New Testament is *eleos* and means "pity" and "compassion." God is the Father of all mercies,[2] has compassion over the works of His Hands,[3] and it is by His mercy that salvation by grace is available.[4] While the grace of God is His goodness applied toward man's debt of sin. God's mercy is His goodness applied toward man's misery.

Because God is a God of love, the Father's tender mercies, eternal and boundless, are brimming with compassion and empathy toward all who would receive Him. The Bible says, *"Surely he has borne our griefs and carried our sorrows."*[5] The cross is good news because not only did grace absolved all our debt, therefore bringing us into right relationship with God, but mercy has removed all our sorrows, therefore making us whole. The Bible says, "*He used his servant body to carry our sins to the Cross so we could be rid of sin, free to live the right way. His wounds became your healing.*"[6]

God's heart towards us is that we would find healing. The Heavenly Father does not delight to see His children merely forgiven yet still hurting. His will is that we should be made whole from all guilt and shame. The beauty of inner wholeness is that it doesn't depend on us. Our healing was made possible at Calvary. We just need to receive it. Mercy is a restorative gift freely available to every son and daughter of God.

Suffering a Part of Life

How does God's tender mercies and desire to see us made whole relate to our experience in a world continuously filled with grief? One does not need to look too far to read, hear, see, or personally experience suffering. While many have objected the goodness of God because pain and suffering even exists, they fail to realize that suffering is a necessary part of life. To use the words of C.S. Lewis, "Try to exclude the possibility of suffering which the order of nature and the existence of free-wills involve, and you find that you have excluded life itself."[7] Put another way, without free will, love would be disingenuous because love demands choice. When we choose God's way, we choose love. When we do not choose God's way, we open the realm of potential for great suffering. The implications of this diametric was made plain from the very beginning when Adam and Eve chose their way rather than God's.

Victorious Living

The Christian life is about victorious living. We live in victory because there is now no condemnation for those who are in Christ.[8] All our guilt, shame and suffering has been absolved by the cross. We are now seen as holy and blameless before Him.[9]

While many have come to know and experience His tender mercies and restorative power, sadly, there are others who lack this experience. They feel oppressed and broken and are unsure if they will ever find rest for their aching soul. Much of the time this is so because they are holding on to pain rather than releasing it. Many prefer to be comforted by the familiarity of suffering rather than know and experience the true freedom of His mercy. Perhaps this is so because they are afraid of the unknown. Could it be that while the Father waits for one to respond in simple, childlike faith, that failure to secure refreshment and healing is the result of lack of knowledge or unbelief? If one could but know and believe that the mercy of God is an unchanging, eternal attribute, teeming with unconditional love, perhaps they would turn and receive the reservoir of mercies that await.

In speaking to the people of His day, Jesus knew that many in Jerusalem would refuse to turn and know true life. They were like the chicks that refused to find solace under the wings of the hen. Jesus said, "*How often I wanted to gather your children together the way a hen gathers her chicks under her wings! But you were not willing!*"[10] Though Jesus has the power to wash away all our sorrows, it does not mean that God will bring wholeness simply because we believe in Him. No, we must let go of our suffering and cling to His comfort and healing. We must find solace under the care of His wings. The Bible says, "*Turn to me and have mercy on me, as you always do to those who love your name.*"[11]

Taking It Home

Every day we must remind our self that every human being is fighting a battle we are unaware of. Some of our battles are easier to detect than others, but we all have them. Regardless of what season you or another are in, we all need to show mercy. The Bible says, "*Be merciful, just as your Father is merciful.*"[12]

What does mercy, therefore, look like in relationship? It is extending kindness and forgiveness, even when we are the one who was offended. Taking the time out of our busy schedule to help another in need. Sacrificing our own resources for the betterment of someone else. Building up another even if they are in the wrong so that they may see the love of God. Responding with patience and care instead of a brash action or word. Simply said mercy is demonstrating the goodness of God toward another especially when they are suffering.

When we apply mercy in relationship, we not only reflect God's character we also open our heart to becoming more Christlike. God wired us so that our external actions impact the inner attitude of our heart. The more we serve and care for others the greater our hearts will expand for God and others. Jesus said, "*For your heart will always pursue what you value as your treasure.*"[13] If we treasure people the heart will follow. This principle also works the other way. When we do not treasure people, our hearts will grow cold. The condition of the heart always reflects one's life. Scripture says, "*As water reflects the face, so one's life reflects the heart.*"[14]

Endless mercies from God's presence await yet we must believe and know that they are there and accessible by faith. To trust in Jesus for salvation and forgiveness yet live a lifetime of unbelief of inner restoration is to beg for crumbs from the King's banquet when we are already a prized and royal family members invited to dine. We must let go of that which weighs us down and take hold of the that which is ours in Christ. God does not hide Himself. The presence of His throne and glorious light is always set before us and mercy and truth are His attendants.[15]

DAY 25

The Mercy of God

MAIN IDEA: Infinite mercy may be found in His presence.

VERSE TO REMEMBER: "*So let us come boldly to the very throne of God and stay there to receive his mercy and to find grace to help us in our times of need.*" Hebrews 4:16 (TLB)

QUESTION TO ASK: What area of my life do I need God's mercy?

Infinite mercy, tender love,
God's goodness, came from above;
By the cross, You nailed my guilt and shame,
Freedom and healing,
In Jesus Name.

DAY 26

THE LOVE OF GOD

Give thanks to the God of heaven! His love is eternal.
PSALM 136:26 (HCSB)

But God's mercy is so abundant, and his love for us is so great, that while we were spiritually dead in our disobedience he brought us to life with Christ.
EPHESIANS 2:4-5A (GNT)

God's love is eternally set apart.

While the love that human beings naturally show one another is conditional and subject to change, God's love is unconditional and never changes. God does not love us because we are lovable or because there is something He sees in us. Nor does He love because we make Him feel good. God loves because love is who He is.

God is Love

Writing as he was carried along by the Spirit, the apostle John wrote that *"God is love."*[1] Many have mistakenly understood this verse to be an absolute statement about the nature of

God, believing that love is literally what God is, rather than an essential attribute that is true of Him. If God is literally love, then we would all be worshipping the attribute of love itself, rather than God Himself. Not only so, but we would be forced to worship but one attribute, for love would be all God is.

The proper way to understand the love of God, therefore, is to view it as an expression of who God is in His unitary nature along with His other attributes.

The *Hesed* and *Agape* Love of God

In the Old Testament, the word that is used most often for God's love is *hesed.* Like other Hebrew words, it signifies action. The *hesed* love of God is tied to covenantal relationship. Because God has bound Himself to His people, He is completely faithful to His self-commitment. God is steadfast, loyal, and true. He graciously intervenes, rescuing and delivering the objects of His covenantal love. *Hesed* is so enduring that is perseveres past sin or betrayal to restore brokenness by extending generous mercy. Because God's is unequivocally faithful, His covenantal love endures forever. The Bible says, "'*The mountains may move, and the hills may shake, but my kindness will never depart from you. My promise of peace will never change," says the LORD, who has compassion on you.*'"[2]

In the New Testament, the Greek word used for God's love is *agape.* In contrast to other New Testament Greek words for love — *phileo* which refers to brotherly love in friendship, and *aeros* which refers to physical love between a husband and wife — God's *agape* love is self-sacrificial and unconditional. God's love for us is so generous that He offered His only Son so that we may receive life eternal. Since God is eternal and infinite, He can give

His love fully and completely to each one. "God loves each of us as if there were only one of us to love," [3] said Saint Augustine.

Receiving God's Love

There are times it is difficult for us to fully accept God's *hesed* and *agape* love, for we are often troubled in mind and heart. Though our faith rises toward His celestial presence, our conscience often weighs heavy. We are daily torn between the upper rise of faith and the burden of fear and know there is nothing a Holy and perfect God sees in us that would merit His compassion. Yet, even in our shortcoming there is absolutely nothing we can do to make God love us any more or any less. God's love knows no bounds. Because this is so, the love of God ought to take away every fear. Because we live in the love of the Father, the Son, and the Holy Spirit, whom or what shall we fear? The Bible says, "*So why would I fear the future? For your goodness and love pursue me all the days of my life. Then afterward, when my life is through, I'll return to your glorious presence to be forever with you!*" [4]

When one receives God's love, the soul comes alive for they can't help but leap with gladness for newness of life. This is so because divine love has regenerative and transformative power. Countless times in the gospels we read people whose lives were touched by Jesus. Every one of them walked away a restored, new person. The same life-changing power is available for us today by faith. Since Jesus Christ is the same yesterday, today, and tomorrow, His love does not change but will always be there to envelope us in His infinite grace and mercy.

Regardless of how long one has walked by faith, the garment of God's *hesed* and *agape* love never wears out. For you will find this garment to be a radiant, abiding source of strength for each day and bright hope for tomorrow. Scripture says, "*He has torn the veil and lifted from me the sad heaviness of mourning. He wrapped me in the glory garments of gladness.*"[5]

Taking It Home

Jesus said that He came to seek and save those who are lost[6] and that He would make His disciples fishers of men.[7] Part of and reaching and saving the lost is loving unconditionally — even if they are hard to love. While this is unnatural in our normal state, the grace of the Holy Spirit enables you to truly love from the heart. Jesus said, "*But I tell you, love your enemies. Pray for those who treat you badly. If you do this, you will be children who are truly like your Father in heaven.*"[8]

Hesed and *agape* love are hallmarks of those who know God and is the essence of the Christian faith. The garment of God's love frees us to now love another human being sincerely. It extends the same love God showed us. It allows us to forgive from the heart for we have been forgiven. It enables us to go the extra mile with joy for God went the distance for us in Christ. It strengthens us during life's trials and tribulations for Jesus endured on our behalf. It comforts us when we experience deep pain and loss, for the Son of Man suffered that we might have life.

Faith is always known by its fruit and "*by their fruit you will know them*"[9] Jesus said. Because God is eternally faithful, steadfast, sacrificial, and merciful, we are to be as well. If the love of the Father is not in us, how shall we say that we are His? The Bible says, "*For love is supreme and must flow through each of these virtues. Love becomes the mark of true maturity.*"[10]

In all things, whether death or life, good report or bad report, the love of God will always prevail. For we are children of the King and immensely loved.

DAY 26

The Love of God

MAIN IDEA: God's love is demonstrated best in Christ.

VERSE TO REMEMBER: *"But God's mercy is so abundant, and his love for us is so great, that while we were spiritually dead in our disobedience he brought us to life with Christ."* Ephesians 2:4-5 (GNT)

QUESTION TO ASK: How can love others with the same love God has given me in Christ?

Infinite, abounding love,
Reaching the heavens, stretching the sky;
You thought of me, in sending Your Son,
Salvation, love immeasurably won.

DAY 27

THE FAITHFULNESS OF GOD

You demonstrate your faithfulness to all generations.
You established the earth and it stood firm.
PSALM 119:90 (NET BIBLE)

Let us hold on firmly to the hope we profess, because
we can trust God to keep his promise.
HEBREWS 10:23 (GNT)

GOD IS UNASSAILABLY TRUSTWORTHY AND TRUE.

There is no might, no power, nor force in hell, on earth, or in heaven that can bend or alter the faithfulness of The Almighty. Before Him the mountains shake, demons run and flee, darkness is vanquished, and Satan is destroyed. Just as the veracity of God is purest truth, so too the faithfulness of God is the firmest and securest reality in all existence. The faithfulness of God is a mighty fortress.

Unshaken Faith

Because God is faithful, He is consistently true to His Word and His promises. Scripture says, "...*He remains faithful, for He cannot deny Himself."*[1] The rock-solid reliability of God's nature gives us great confidence before Him. We know that all God has decreed shall come to pass and that God is who His Word says He is.

The implication of God's faithfulness deduces that He is therefore faithful in all His holy attributes. The knowledge of the holy that dwells in the deepest part of the soul can only come about by total sureness of His faithfulness. Speaking of the certitude we have in God and His promises, Scripture says, *"Now faith is the assurance that what we hope for will come about and the certainty that what we cannot see exists."*[2] Assurance of what we hope for and certainty of what we do not see are not possibilities or potentials, they are guarantees and absolutes. Though faith does not see physically, it perceives by the heart; though faith does not fully comprehend, it trusts by the Spirit.

God is Faithful to Keep Us Blameless

One of the most beautiful promises in all of God's Word relates to the conservation those who are His. Because God is faithful, it is He alone who will keep us from stumbling and to present us without fault and with great joy.[3] It is He alone who will preserve our faith all the days of our life. The Bible says, *"May he keep your whole being — spirit, soul, and body — blameless when our Lord Jesus Christ comes. The one who calls you is faithful, and he will do this."*[4] While we are responsible to live a pure and holy life before God, never forget that all things come through God, including our own ability to have faith in Him to begin with.[5] While the paradox of God's sovereignty and man's responsibility is incomprehensible, it is true nevertheless; God alone keeps us holy. So, while pureness and blamelessness have nothing to do with us and everything to do with God, we are responsible to obey the Spirit.

Because God is faithful, not only are we declared to be pure and blameless before Him, but our identity can never be shaken. In Christ, we are chosen and adopted as a son or a daughter, have received the promised Holy Spirit, are a valued part of His heavenly kingdom and have the assurance of eternal glory.[6] If the King of the universe has decreed these truths who or what shall undo them?

God's Faithfulness in Dry and Difficult Seasons

We all experience seasons of life that are trying. In those times, choosing to believe that God is faithful or that our identity in Him hasn't been stained can be very difficult. Our faith most certainly will be tested. Unexplainable experiences in life will happen. There will be moments that may be so dark that we can hardly sense a trace of God. There will also be days we wake up and do not feel like much of a Christian or a Christian at all. Sometimes these are due to "dry seasons;" other times they are caused by habitual sin, and still other times they are caused by intense sorrow which can deaden and numb the soul. In those moments, sin and evil will be crouching at the door,[7] waiting to twist and confuse truth, thereby clouding the conscious with doubt and distrust. Eyes will be full of tears and whispers from the enemy will slowly creep in sowing lies and accusations to destroy everything good in your life. When those moments come remember this prevailing saying: *Don't doubt in the dark what God revealed to you in the light.*[8] God is faithful. His perfect grace will find a way to lift you up. His tender mercies will bring healing. His love will surround you. His truth will gleam into those deepest, darkest parts of life and bring beauty from the ashes.

Taking It Home

You see friend, God has always been there. From beginning to end He is the Author and the Sustainer of your life. Before you were born, you were known and loved by God. He formed you in your mother's womb[9] and has been there every day of your life. He holds you in the palm of His Hand. Because His Word is trustworthy and true and His character consistent and dependable your identity is secure in Him. Nothing in all creation shall bend or alter what God has decreed over your life. He is our mighty fortress and our great and mighty King showing His faithfulness to a thousand generations who love Him and keep His Word.[10]

DAY 27

The Faithfulness of God

MAIN IDEA: God is always trustworthy and true.

VERSE TO REMEMBER: "*Let us hold firmly to the hope we profess, because we can trust God to keep his promise.*" Hebrews 10:23 (GNT)

QUESTION TO ASK: In what ways do I see God's faithfulness in my life?

As the sun rises each morning,
So too You are faithful each day;
Your character is consistent,
Your nature never changes,
Teach me to be like You,
To reflect Your faithfulness.

DAY 28

THE JUSTICE OF GOD

But let justice run down like water, And righteousness like a mighty stream.
AMOS 5:24 (NKJV)

He has shown you, O mortal, what is good. And what does the LORD require of you? To act justly and to love mercy and to walk humbly with your God.
MICAH 6:8 (NIV)

THE JUSTICE OF GOD EMBODIES HIS MORAL RULE IN the universe.

On the day of judgment, all things are weighed against God's character. Whatever is not found to be of His character will be deemed, as the writing on the wall in Daniel 5, to be weighed and measured, and found wanting.

God is the standard by which all things are measured not only because He is the Author of Life, but because His character is infinitely true. Therefore, lying is wrong because God is truth; killing is wrong because God is life; and stealing is wrong because God's way is that of integrity. Thus, when God reproves sin or rewards the upright, He upholds the truth of His character.

God's Weighs the Intent of the Heart

The reality is every human being naturally behaves in a manner that seems upright to themselves. In the end, however, God weighs the true intent of our heart. The Bible says, *"All a person's ways seem pure to them, but motives are weighed by the LORD."* [1]

While God is the standard by which all things are weighed, the *scale* God uses to weigh all things is the truth of His Word. The Bible says that God's Word is sharper than a double-edged sword and so precise that it pierces through where soul and spirit meet, evaluating every slight desire and motive, including hidden things which one may not be conscious of.[2] Well-aware of this and knowing he carried countless hidden faults, King David cried out, *"Who perceives his unintentional sins? Cleanse me from my hidden faults."* [3]

Erroneous Views of Justice

Many today hold erroneous views of the justice of God. They maintain that truth is relative, that God is too kind and too loving to punish sin, and that the Bible is too extreme. They diminish sin to the point where the only remnant of sin in our society is that which is labeled "crime," all else is personal opinion and dare not be judged. Morality has become associated with whatever is socially or civilly acceptable instead of what God's Word declares as true. Man, rather than God, has become the standard by which all things are weighed. If one is an upstanding, law abiding citizen one is perceived as basically good. This subterfuge of thought permits an excess of sin, pacifying and dulling the conscience, all the while death and judgment looms nearer each day.

When one thinks about it, how else must God respond? There are only five possibilities when it comes to sin: God is either entirely unaware of it, deliberately chooses to ignore it, mildly rebukes it, weighs the good versus the bad, or hates it with an eternal, holy detestation. The first cannot be true because God is omniscient. The second and third cannot be true because God is consistent in His character and dealing with men. The fourth cannot be possible because the Bible declares that even our most righteous deeds are but filthy rags[4] and that no one does good, not even one.[5] The latter is the only possible reality because God is perfectly Holy. Therefore, we must learn to see sin the same as God sees it.

Justice and the Goodness of God

The reality is that many, including sincere believers in Christ, cringe at the thought of God's eternal wrath. Though we have the Holy Spirit of God, the sinful nature is constantly battling for our mind, will, and emotions — ever seeking to distort and disfigure our knowledge of the Holy One. We must remind our self that whatever God does is good — and when He judges, we can trust His goodness in His judgment — even when we don't understand.

Regardless of whether society chooses to accept or reject God's justice or His holy wrath toward sin, God's truth will prevail. The Almighty shall someday be proved right when He speaks and justified when He judges.[6] The Bible says, "*Let God be true, and every human being a liar.*"[7] One day all created beings in heaven and on earth — including those who have long passed — will bow in worship before Jesus Christ and declare Him King of kings and Lord of lords.[8]

Taking It Home

In light of God's justice and the eternal weight of glory, how can we better apply the truth of God's justice here and now?

First, as an imitator of Jesus Christ, remind our self that part of following God is loving what is just. How can we truly say we love God if we lack the desire to see people treated fairly? Just the same, how is the love of God in us if we lack the integrity to stand for what is just — even if it means showing fairness to the very person or group that treated us poorly to begin with? God's love is not an eye for an eye or a tooth,[9] but means going the extra mile[10] and praying for those who mistreat us.[11] The Bible says, *"He has shown you, O mortal, what is good. And what does the LORD require of you? To act justly and to love mercy and to walk humbly with your God."*[12]

Second, every believer in Christ is called to heroically display the justice of God in all the earth. While every generation faces its own injustices and it will always be this way until Jesus returns, we are nevertheless called by God to free those wrongly imprisoned, to let the oppressed go free, and to remove the chains that bind people.[13] This takes courage. Unfortunately, many are unwilling to put their life or reputation on the line for fear of what may happen or what others may think. May this never said of God's people.

Third, God alone makes the wrongs right. It is not ours to repay. Even when others sin against us, we are to treat people with dignity, respect, and equality, for all are created in God's image. We must remember that we will be held accountable for how we react or respond. If this is an area that we struggle in, we must not be afraid to ask God for wisdom or to expand our heart.

Lastly, we should live with great anticipation because of the hope we profess! We have much to look forward to in Christ, more than we can now grasp. Someday, God will make all the wrongs right. The suffering of the believers shall be justified, freedom will reign, unending peace with God will endure, everlasting joy will runoff, and every tear wiped from our eyes[14] — and that because God is just.

DAY 28

The Justice of God

MAIN IDEA: God's character is the standard by which all things are weighed.

VERSE TO REMEMBER: *"He has shown you, O mortal, what is good. And what does the LORD require of you? To act justly and to love mercy and to walk humbly with your God."*
Micah 6:8 (NIV)

QUESTION TO ASK: In what ways can I act more justly, love mercy, and walk humbly with God?

O Sovereign Lord,

Your justice is perfect, And Your scales precise,

Christ, my great substitute, God's wrath You did suffice;

May I learn Your justice, And exemplify Your ways,

Freedom from captivity, God's goodness on display.

DAY 29

THE JOY OF GOD

Your presence is fullness of joy; At Your right hand are pleasures forevermore.
PSALM 16:11B (NKJV)

In God's kingdom, what we eat and drink is not important. Here is what is important: a right way of life, peace, and joy — all from the Holy Spirit.
ROMANS 14:17 (ERV)

THE JOY OF THE LORD SUPERSEDES ALL CIRCUMSTANCE and emotion.

All of us experience the daily reality of the ups and the downs. It is easy to let these experiences navigate our thinking. When things are going well, we often have greater satisfaction and contentment. When things are not well it is easier to become dissatisfied and discontent. Though God created us to have and express our emotion, God does not desire that our emotions control our life. This is where the joy of the Lord comes in. As one of the fruits of the Holy Spirit, joy freely gives something the circumstances of life never could — true contentment. Joy is an anchor that is rooted in God's promises and the river of life that gives one the ability to rejoice under trials. The joy of God is not an emotion, but it is a deeper, inner sense of peace, comfort, and encouragement from the Holy Spirit. Joy is supernatural, for it supersedes all experience. It is permanent, for the child of God need but lift their eyes to the Father to find strength, contentment, and inspiration. It is effervescent, for it gives good cheer regardless of circumstance. Truly the joy of the Lord is our strength.[1]

Unfortunately, many in the church today lack joy. Whatever the reason — the feeling of defeat, fatigue, or complacency — the joy of God is often missing. This is a sad reality! Perhaps this is so because of incorrectly equating joy with the emotional state of happiness. Once this mistake is made, one is at the mercy of their own circumstance or emotion, ever thrown back and forth like the waves of the seas. When joy is properly understood, however, the waves of life suddenly become calm as the soul is anchored to the Living God.

Perspective Gives Joy

Because joy comes from trusting God, even if we do not know what the present or the future holds, we can persevere through difficult times. How do we know these things to be true? Because Scripture reveals that God is working all things to form godliness into our life[2] and to refine our faith.[3] When the mind and heart accepts this perspective, the Holy Spirit imparts a sense of inner contentment, enabling our faith to grow. The Bible says, *"Dear brothers and sisters, when troubles of any kind come your way, consider it an opportunity for great joy. For you know that when your faith is tested, your endurance has a chance to grow. So let it grow, for when your endurance is fully developed, you will be perfect and complete, needing nothing.”*[4]

In the book of Acts, when Paul and Silas were severely flogged, thrown into an inner prison cell, and shackled at their feet for the testimony of Jesus, they did not shrink back or lose heart. Instead, they prayed and sang hymns to God! How could they have had such remarkable joy in a dark, forsaken moment? In the eyes of the world having joy in this circumstance would be deranged. But for Paul and Silas God was in control. They knew that their momentary circumstance was an opportunity to give God glory and to witness to those around them. As they prayed and sang, a great earthquake shook, and the prison doors opened. When the guard saw what happened he was greatly troubled and asked what he must do to be saved. At that very hour the guard and his entire household believed upon the Lord Jesus, were baptized, and filled with great joy.[5]

While there are many lessons we can learn from this story, two stand out. The first is that Paul and Silas maintained steadfast perspective under suffering, and because they did so they had great joy. The second is that God was able to use their joy amidst their circumstance as a powerful testimony and witness to those around them. Let us never forget that God can use all things for His purposes — including impacting others through the joy we have in God amidst tough circumstances.

God’s Presence Brings Fullness of Joy

The ultimate example of how to endure through trial and tribulation and do so with great joy is our Lord and Savior. The Bible teaches that Jesus was the suffering servant who gave His life as an offering for sin,[6] and for the joy set before Him endured its suffering and shame.[7] What was this joy which was set before Him? Was it not the joy of bringing the Father great glory in reconciling your soul back to God? Was it not the joy of creating one new people out of the nations of the world? This joy was not one-sided, but a joy God's people will share with God for eternity.

The Bible says that to be in the presence of the Savior is to experience incalculable, overwhelming, glorious joy. It is, is in every sense of the word, wholly inexpressible. Someday in heaven, innocence will be restored, the purity of God will radiate from within, without, and around, and everlasting happiness shall run-off as living water. The soul will be fully alive, united with its glorious, incorruptible body, reflecting the brilliance the glory of the Living God.

Though we have not yet experienced these things, we can know the presence of our Savior in this life. There are moments where God's presence is more pronounced and others where it is difficult to sense His nearness, though He is never far off for He never leaves nor forsakes. Either way, the Christian has something the world will never find — true joy. For the world runs after temporary, fleeting pursuits but the joy of God is everlasting.

Just as the presence of The Almighty is the most powerful force in existence, yet calmer and gentler than a dove, so too is the joy of God. It is purest strength, perpetual love and light, and the safest, most secure place.

Taking It Home

The Bible says, *"I keep my eyes always on the LORD. With him at my right hand, I will not be shaken."*[8] The phrase "right hand" appears 166 times in the Bible and signifies the blessing, strength, and the sovereign protection of the Lord. This is an astounding truth, for Jesus presently sits at the right hand of the Father in Heaven, and…so do you! The Bible says, "*God raised us from death to life with Christ Jesus, and he has given us a place beside Christ in heaven.*"[9] If Jesus is seated at the right hand of the Father, and spiritually you are seated next to Christ, what in all existence shall prevail over you? This is why Paul and Silas could so boldly believe that the waves of life have no bearing on the Christian, for neither death nor life, neither angels nor demons, neither the present nor the future, nor any powers, nor anything in creation can triumph over you.[10]

Since we have been raised up with Christ from death unto life and are seated with Him in heaven, we are to set our minds on the things of heaven.[11] Why is this so? Because heaven is our true home and identity. We know there is no hope for this world devoid of the gospel and that everything in the world will someday come to an end. Therefore, let us have tremendous joy because we know that this life is fleeting, and we have an eternal home that awaits.

As children of God we are to invest in that which will last forever, and, my friend, there are only three things that will last forever: *God, God's Word,* and *people.* Let these three be that which we value the most.

DAY 29

The Joy of God

MAIN IDEA: The joy of the Lord supersedes all circumstance and emotion.

VERSE TO REMEMBER: *"In Your presence is fullness of joy; At your right hand are pleasures forevermore."* Psalm 16:11b (NKJV)

QUESTION TO ASK: Is my life marked by joy?

O God, in Your presence is fullness of joy,
And in You do I find true life everlasting;
You rejoice over me, celebrate my faith;
Whether in the calm or in the storm,
I lay anchor in Your Word,
Hold fast to Your Truth;
And find joy in You.

DAY 30

THE PEACE OF GOD

Now may the Lord of peace himself give you his peace at all times and in every situation.
2 THESSALONIANS 3:16A (NLT)

You will keep the mind that is dependent on you in perfect peace, for it is trusting in you.
ISAIAH 26:3A (CSB)

True peace comes through knowing Jesus Christ.

It doesn't take very long to look around and realize that the world is at unrest. We are continuously chasing after that one eluding thing that seems to slip through our fingertips. From new experiences, to a healthier mind and body, to financial security, to improved relationships — all fall short in the quest toward finding what we truly long for — enduring peace. Though these pursuits are quite worthy and even necessary to our basic human needs, they can never satisfy our soul. Jesus knew this truth all too well when He promised His disciples what the world never could, "*I give you peace, the kind of peace only I can give. It isn't like the peace this world can give. So don't be worried or afraid."*[1] Jesus knew the inner quest of the soul ultimately points back to God. He is the Bread of Life and the Living Water which man may eat and never go hungry, or drink and never go thirsty; for through Christ alone man has never-ending fellowship with the Living God.

Peace by Way of the Cross

Peace with God in a picture-perfect world is something humanity once had long ago. The garden was an exquisite paradise where man had direct access to God — audibly! Because of Adam's fall, a perfect oasis was substituted for an arduous life tilling the soul, and instantaneous connection with the Creator was unraveled by spiritual separation from God.

Amidst this great tragedy God rescued us while we were helpless to rescue ourselves. Scripture reveals that in His great love God made us alive when we were dead in our own sins![2] Jesus, our Prince of Peace,[3] bridged the gap between sinful man and a Holy God by making peace through His blood shed on the cross.[4] The apostle Paul heralded this prevailing truth when he penned his letter to the church in Galatia, "*We have been made right with God because of our faith. So we have peace with God through our Lord Jesus Christ.*"[5] Instead of conflict and separation, everlasting peace and connection with God is now possible by way of the cross.

Peace and Joy Marks of Salvation

In the Bible, peace and joy are often used in conjunction with one another as the Holy Spirit strengthens the believer in grace.

Although we are to live in this manner, *what exactly is the difference between peace and joy?* The answer is peace comes from the resolution of a former conflict, whereas joy is underlying contentment amidst hardship. Both are indispensable workings and evidence of the Spirit; for without inner peace and joy our lives would not look any different nor would we truly know whether we belong to God. Scripture reveals, *"Every believer of this good news bears the fruit of eternal life as they experience the reality of God's grace."*[6]

A Man After God's Heart

One of the greatest examples in the Bible of someone who truly experienced peace with God amidst fear is King David. Though admired for his unusual leadership capability and strong courage before God, David still experienced tremendous hardships — some a result of his own doing. In Psalm 23 he wrote, *"The Lord is my best friend and my shepherd. I always have more than enough. He offers a resting place for me in his luxurious love. He takes me to an oasis of peace, the quiet brook of bliss."*[7] How is it that David came to such an oasis of peace with His Lord? Although David was the anointed king of Israel, he experienced seasons where he fled to caves to spare his life from King Saul and even from his own son Absalom after he became king. He also committed grievous sins against God by committing adultery with Bathsheba, the wife of Uriah who was his best soldier, which later lead to Uriah's murder in a scandalous cover up.

Doesn't peace come to those with upright character before God? The Bible tells us that although David was incredibly far from perfect and committed grievous sins, he was, nevertheless, a man after God's own heart.[8] How is this possible? The answer is that David knew he had transgressed against God and formed conflict with God when he committed adultery and murder. He knew that only sincere brokenness and complete repentance could restore his life.[9] While David, with his mix of talent, courage, and clear deficiencies, serves as a principal example of the repentant heart, the enduring lesson we can learn from his story is this: peace with God is not contingent upon how holy we are but upon God's infinite goodness alone.

Experiencing Internal Peace

The goodness of God is not merely something demonstrated through Jesus' death and resurrection two millennia ago, it is something the Christian may experience moment-by-moment. To find inner peace, the Bible says that we must first repent of our sins and place our faith in Jesus Christ. This saving faith brings us into right standing with God. Yet, this is just the beginning of a lifetime journey of knowing and loving God. As His children, we are to lean upon and worship our God daily. The best way to worship is to cultivate the habit of aligning our mind and heart toward His goodness each morning. The Bible teaches that we are to give thanks and rejoice in all settings. When we do this, we attain a peace that exceeds all comprehension.[10] We may not understand our world or how a situation will end up, but we can have peace as sons and daughters.

Therefore, let us learn to submit our desires and persistent want of control over to God. The theological principle of submitting is not only for our encouragement but also a prevailing command in Scripture. Just as God withheld the gift of leading the first generation of Hebrew captives into the promised land due to their continuous grumbling and lack of faith, so we too must be mindful that we are not falling into the same trap.

Let us pause and ask a few candid questions:

"Am I honestly grateful for God's provision in my life?"

"Do I recognize and thank Him for the miracles He has done?"

"Do I rejoice in my God and Savior regardless of hardship?"

While God withheld his people from entering the promised land under Moses' leadership, they never ceased being God's people. It only means that they missed out on the blessing of what could have been the best part of their life — the fulfillment of God's great promise to their forefather Abraham. They were just as loved as their descendants who under Joshua's mantle were finally able to cross the threshold into the land flowing with milk and honey. Nevertheless, their lack of faith and complaining got the best of them. Let us remember that although we belong to Christ our minds and attitudes must remain in check. There is always a strong correlation between the level of faith we have and the level of peace we obtain.

Taking It Home

In Christ we have the promise of eternal peace with God through Jesus' finished work on the cross and we experience this peace through submitting to God. The Enemy stands opposed to both God and His church and constantly assault the peace that we have obtained. The Bible says, "*We are not fighting against humans. We are fighting against forces and authorities and against rulers of darkness and powers in the spiritual world.*" [11] Therefore let us not be unwise: we must be on guard and expect these unseen forces to send doubts, worries, anxieties, and confusion at us to pull us away. The Bible says that we have the power to overcome these anti-Christ forces because the one who is in us is greater than the one who is in the world.[12] To do this we must begin our day by realigning our mind and heart upon God. Pray the armor of God,[13] cast your cares upon Him,[14] and rejoice and give thanks.[15] When we do these things we obtain a peace that acts as a shield.

Finally, let learn to extend the peace of Christ toward our relationships with others. God's Word says, "*Blessed are the peacemakers, for they will be called children of God.*"[16] As a son or daughter of faith, the Bible says that we are to seek to imitate the character of Christ in all things.[17] Just as Jesus made peace between us and God, so too we are to make peace with others through imitating the grace, mercy, and forgiveness of God. While the goodness of God is provisionally different in that He alone could pay for the sins of the world, the principle of reconciliation between one person and another remains. The Bible explains, "*Put up with each other, and forgive anyone who does you wrong, just as Christ has forgiven you.*"[18] Far too often we focus on knowing and serving God but overlook whether we have caused a brother or sister harm. We must learn to leave our gift at the altar, first go and be reconciled to our brother or sister, and then come back and worship God.[19] In so doing we bring great glory to our Heavenly Father and experience the gift of peace earthly relationships bring.

DAY 30

The Peace of God

MAIN IDEA: Peace with God comes through knowing Jesus Christ.

VERSE TO REMEMBER: *"Now may the Lord of peace himself give you his peace at all times and in every situation."*
2 Thessalonians 3:16a (NLT)

QUESTION TO ASK: Do I regularly experience inner peace with God?

God of all peace,
May I walk rightly with You,
Reflecting Your ways,
Trusting Your goodness;
By the cross, peace made possible,
Reconciliation to God
Love inexhaustible.

EPILOGUE

MEDITATING ON GOD'S HOLY ATTRIBUTES

Be still and know that I am God.
PSALM 46:10A (NIV)

I ask that your minds may be opened to see his light,
so that you will know what is the hope to which he has called you,
how rich are the wonderful blessings he promises his people.
EPHESIANS 1:18 (GNT)

LIFE IS NOT ABOUT YOU.

True meditation begins when we stop focusing on our self and start focusing on God. We must learn and accept that we play a very small yet valuable part in God's plan; and that life, including our own existence, is about God and bringing Him glory. Herein lies a fine line: For on the one hand we were created to think, reason, and make decisions for the benefit of our self and the world around us, yet on the other hand we are to make these very choices about God. On the surface, these differing perspectives seem to contradictory yet at the root they ought to be one and the same.

When God created Adam and Eve, He blessed them told them to be fruitful and multiply, to fill the earth and to rule over it.[1] The mandate was not about the man or the woman, but about God. In living it out they would fulfill their God-given purpose. In other words, by doing what they were created to do Adam and Eve would point to the greatness of their Creator. The fall spoiled this vision. Instead of making life about God, the rebellion altered not only Adam and Eve's perception of God but humanity's perception of the mandate as well. No longer would life be about God and His glory, but about building a life and name for ourselves.

The mantra *"For yours is the kingdom and the glory and the power forever"*[2] became *"For ours is the kingdom and the glory and the power forever."* From the Towel of Babel, to the great Assyrian and Babylonian empires, to the Greek and Roman rule, every generation great and small has naturally sought out to make a name for itself. The same is true for us. Are we not predisposed toward arguing with God tooth and nail when things do not go our way? Do we not naturally make decisions that ultimately look out for our own interests above another? Our sinful nature is difficult to shake. Indeed, it cannot be shaken unless the Spirit of God continually renews and transforms our mind and heart. In order to come to that place, we must regularly surrender our desire for control.

Be Still and Know that I am God

The Bible says, *"Be still, and know that I am God."*[3] While many Christians have interpreted this verse to mean "be quiet before God," or "make time for God," the meaning of this verse is actually very different. The Hebrew term used here for "be still" is "*harpū*" and means "to let go," "cease striving," and "become helpless." In other words, "*Let go* and know that I am God," "*Cease striving* and know that I am God," or "*Become helpless* and know that I am God."

Just as a seed must fall to the ground and die to its shell in order to produce fruit, so too we must die to our self in order to live for God. This was one of Jesus' central teachings, for a man or woman shall never enter the kingdom of God unless they are born again.[4] In one of His parables, Jesus compared the act of dying to self and living for God to a single kernel of wheat that died to its shell so that it might produce many new kernels, bearing a plentiful harvest. Using this analogy, Jesus then said, *"In the same way, anyone who holds on to life just as it is destroys that life. But if you let it go, reckless in your love, you'll have it forever, real and eternal."*[5] The act of dying to this world is more than initial repentance and belief in Jesus Christ, but a daily, moment-by-moment conscious choice of letting go and realizing our helplessness before God. Until we die to our selfish, proud nature we cannot bear fruit unto God, much less truly known Him.

Renewal of the Mind

Transformation begins with a conscious renewal of the mind. The Bible says, *"Don't copy the behavior and customs of this world, but let God transform you into a new person by changing the way you think."*[6] Our external actions directly flow from the internal state of our mind, and the state of our mind is a direct result of our moment-by-moment mental choices. Like any habit the more we choose God the easier it will become to choose God. Consistent choices add up even if we cannot remember all of them. We may not remember everything we ate yesterday, last week, or last month, but it doesn't mean it hasn't impacted the state of our physical health today. The same is true spiritually, mentally, and emotionally. Our present condition is very much impacted by the choices we made yesterday, last week, or last month.

Our present condition also stems from how we choose to spend the moments of solitude we had *and* the time we spent with others. What did we fill our mind with when we had alone time? What things did we talk about when we were with others? These choices and more impact our inner world. All of us are malleable. God alone is unmalleable. The Bible says, "*Do not be misled: "Bad company corrupts good character."*"[7]

Meditation on God is both an art and a science. It is an art because there is no one right way to meditate upon His glory and splendor. No two people have the same personality or way of processing. It is also a science because God has gifted His children with the same methods to get to know Him, namely: *The Holy Scriptures*, *the Holy Spirit*, *fellowship with like-minded Christians*, *serving others*, and *worship through music*. Each one of these provides a unique spiritual benefit.

The Holy Scriptures

Jesus taught that man should not live by bread alone but every Word that comes from the mouth of God. Without the Scriptures we would not know God's plan of salvation or what His character is like.

God's truth should not merely be read through but processed. Take time to think, pray, and ponder what we are reading. Just as God designed a cow with four stomachs to help process food, so too we should constantly chew and process on God's truth — over and over. The more we take time to meditate in this manner the more blessed and fruitful our lives will become. The Bible says, *"Instead you thrill to GOD's Word, you chew on Scripture day and night. You're a tree replanted in Eden, bearing fresh fruit every month, Never dropping a leaf, always in blossom."* [8]

The Holy Spirit

The Holy Spirit helps illuminate the truth of God so that it shines within our hearts. Jesus said, *"But when he, the Spirit of truth, comes, he will guide you into all the truth."* [9]

Scripture teaches that our natural mind is opposed to God's truth because it desires what is opposite of God. As you meditate on God's Word, pray and ask the Spirit to cleanse your thoughts so you can know God's character and nature better. Ask the Spirit to help you remember the truths He reveals to you and to engrave those truths on the tablet of your heart.

Fellowship with Like-Minded Christians

We must learn to surround our self with like-minded Christians who also want to know God in a deeper, more meaningful way. The spiritual life cannot be lived alone. As branches cannot live without the vine, so too we cannot live without being connected to Christ's body, the church.

Many Christians are surface deep, lack hunger, or a purposeful desire to draw closer to God. Because of this, many remain lukewarm and want to be fed instead of learning how to feed themselves. While we are to be on mission to build up our brothers and sisters and help them see God, we must be careful that we aren't surrounding our self with lukewarm Christians too much since they will lessen the temperature of our desire for God. Lukewarmness within the church stems not only from the shallow spirituality of each individual but the content of their conversations when the church gathers together. Do our conversations edify and build one another up or are they unspiritual and worldly? Scripture make it very clear, "*Avoid godless chatter, because those who indulge in it will become more and more ungodly.*"[10]

Serving Others

Expect God to place opportunities across your path to impact another person — whether through your words, actions, or just listening. Words have the power to lovingly build up, actions can meet a deep need, and a sympathetic, listening ear can calm the cares of another.

In the Parable of the Sheep and the Goats, Jesus taught that all who truly know God (the Sheep) sincerely serve the needs of others, particularly those less fortunate. Jesus said that any time they did these things they did so unto Him. Mother Teresa of Calcutta said it this way, "Each one of them is Jesus in His most distressing disguise."[11] The astonishing thing about the parable is that God's people did not even realize they were serving Jesus when they cared for the needs of others. Their actions were simply an overflow of their heart. Jesus informed that serving should be a very natural part of life, and our faith: "*But when you give to the needy, do not let your left hand know what your right hand is doing.*"[12]

Worship Through Music

Music is powerful and has a profound ability to impact our mind, heart, and emotions. Like many things in life, music can either draw us closer to God or pull us away from Him. We must be intentional about what we are filling our minds with. When King David meditated on God, he often did so through writing and song. He said, *"I will praise the LORD with all my life; I will sing praises to my God as long as I live."*[13]

Not only does music draw your mind and heart closer God, it also wards off the Enemy. The spiritual, unseen realm is the real reality. We mustn't forget that our true battle is against unseen forces. One of the reasons why music is so powerful is because we are blocking out the Enemy through using many of our senses simultaneously. When we read, we only use our eyes. When we listen, we only use our ears. But when we worship God through song, we are using our mouth, our ears, and our emotions. We are also declaring truth in the spiritual realm. Since we are seated next to Christ in heaven, we have the authority in Jesus Name to declare victory over the Enemy!

Taking It Home

While God has blessed the church with a variety of means to know and worship Him, the fundamental principle remains that *we must Seek God first above all.* We must seek the Giver more than the gift. The Merciful and Compassionate Father more than His mercy and compassion. The God of Justice more than His justice. The Lord of Peace more than His peace. The Joyful One more than His joy. And the Forgiver more than His forgiveness. For in so doing all these things shall be added unto us as well.

Meditating on God's Holy Attributes

MAIN IDEA: True meditation begins when we stop focusing on our self and begin focusing on God.

VERSE TO REMEMBER: *"Be still and know that I am God."* Psalm 46:10a (NIV)

QUESTION TO ASK: In what ways can I better focus my life around God?

Almighty God, Lord of all things,
You reveal Yourself to the Humble,
Those who seek Your face shall find;
I worship You alone, You alone do I seek;
May I hunger and thirst for righteousness,
For Your Kingdom come.

APPENDIX

Definitions and Concepts

Agape: The self-sacrificial, unconditional love of God toward humanity. God's agape love is best demonstrated through the sacrifice of His Son, Jesus Christ, for the sins of the world.

Almighty: A name for God that comes from the Hebrew expression "*Shaddai*" and means "all-powerful." The name is always in connection with the Almighty's promises to His people and implies that He can do everything He promised. The name is also associated by the Psalmist as One in whom complete rest and safety are found.

Angels: Faithful messengers of God who serve the Lord and look after God's people.

Anthropomorphism: The attribution of human qualities and characteristics in describing God to be more understandable and relatable to the reader.

Attribute of God: That which God has revealed as true of Himself — the qualities ofGod that constitute who He is in His basic character and nature.

Calvary: The hill near Jerusalem where Jesus was crucified. The word comes from the Latin "*calvaria*" which means "a skull" and is also called "Golgotha." Calvary is associated as a place of suffering.

Character of God: The moral qualities of God; namely purity, integrity, and goodness.

Children of God: Those who have placed their faith in Jesus Christ and are therefore adopted into God's family, the church.

Consuming Fire: A description of God depicting the nature of His Holiness manifested in judgment.

Contemplation: The art and science of pondering the character and nature of God, as well as His roles, divine acts, and promises.

Deity of Christ: The divine nature of the Second Person of the Holy Trinity, Jesus Christ, who is fully God, co-equal with the Father and the Holy Spirit, and worthy of all worship and adoration.

Demons: Evil, deceiving spiritual forces who stand in hostility to God.

Depravity: The completely crooked and helpless nature of humanity. Human beings are totally unable to forgive, change, or redeem themselves from their fallen condition. The term depravity is derived from two Latin words: *de* meaning "completely" and *pravus* meaning "crooked."

Dunamis: The Greek New Testament word that refers to the inherent ability, might, strength power, moral power, or miraculous power of God in and through the life of the believer.

Economic Trinity: The theological term that describes the unique relationship of the Father, the Son, and the Holy Spirit. While each Person of the Holy Trinity are one in divinity, their roles and function in relation to one another are different. The term "economic" comes from the Greek word *oikonomia*, which means "household management." The "economy" of a household includes designated roles within the family.

Eternity: Having no beginning and no end. Timeless.

Eternal Condemnation: A state of permanent, everlasting punishment for those who reject the gift of God's Son, Jesus Christ.

Ex Nihilo: A Latin phrase that means "out of nothing." God, who is Spirit, spoke and created physical existence out of nothing.

Faith: The assurance in God's promises and certainty of what is not seen.

Faithfulness of God: The flawless reliability of God to Himself, His Word, and His promises.

Forgiveness: The action or process of permanently: 1) canceling a debt for an offense or mistake, and 2) casting away all anger or resentment.

General Revelation: Knowledge about God that may be obtained through natural means such as creation, philosophy, and reason. General revelation is enough to condemn humanity but insufficient to save.

Glorification: The final state of salvation for the believer. The Bible teaches that all believers shall not only see Christ in His heavenly glory but shall share glory with Christ for all eternity. Glorification includes the receiving of a new, uncorruptible heavenly body and permanence with God forevermore.

Good Works: Actions, attitudes, motives, and words that bring honor and glory to God. Good works always flow out of love toward God and people. Good works in and of themselves do not save. They are a heartfelt response of gratitude for the salvation and grace one has received.

Goodness of God: That which leads God to be benevolent, and compassionate toward His creation. It is most effectively demonstrated in his moral attributes of grace, mercy, faithfulness, justice, and the multifaceted characteristics that are identified as his love.

Grace of God: The goodness of God applied toward our demerit and debt.

Harpu: A Hebrew term that means "to let go," "cease striving," and "become helpless."

Heaven: The dwelling place of God and the angels that is distinct from the earth. It is also the place where believers will receive their eternal reward.

Hell: An eternal place of suffering for those who reject Jesus Christ.

Hesed: A Hebrew word that signifies the covenantal relationship of God with His people. Hesed is characterized best as the complete faithfulness, trustworthiness, and loyalty of God.

Holiness of God: The completely set apart character and nature of God that is entirely other than.

Holy Fear: A reverent, healthy respect for the Holiness of God.

Holy of Holies: The earthly dwelling place of God on earth in the Old Testament. Under the new covenant of Christ, God's dwelling is now within the temple of our bodies by faith in Jesus Christ.

Holy Spirit: The Third Person of the Holy Trinity. The Holy Spirit is known as our Helper, the Spirit of Truth, and God's deposit guaranteeing our eternal inheritance in His kingdom.

Holy Trinity: The name for the three Persons who make up the Godhood: The Father, The Son, and The Holy Spirit. God is three-in-one and one-in-three.

Humanity: Human beings whom God made in His image. Originally created to live with God perfectly, presently fallen because of sin, and in need of God's forgiveness and grace.

Humanity of Christ: The human nature of the Second Person of the Holy Trinity, Jesus Christ, who was fully human and experienced the same things we experience including the temptations of sin yet was without sin.

Identity in Christ: Who God says you are based on the truth of His Word. All who arein Christ have become a new person.

Idolatry: The worship of something or someone other than God. Idols can be concrete, such as people or things; or abstract, such as mental concepts or ideas.

Illumination: The active role of the Holy Spirit that opens the spiritual eyes of the believer to see and understand God's truth as revealed through His written Word.

Imago Dei: The image or likeness of God in human beings; including man's soul, rationality, mind, will, emotions, and personhood.

Immanence: The active presence and participation of God in creation.

Immutability: The unchanging character and nature of God.

Impeccability: The flawless perfection of God in His character and nature, as well as His acts.

Imputation: The non-experiential act whereby God imputes contingent holiness through faith in Christ's shed blood.

Incarnation: The uniting of God and humanity into one individual existence by the virgin birth. Jesus Christ is fully God and fully man.

Incomprehensibility: The inability of created human beings to fully comprehend or describe the uncreated God.

Infallibility of Scripture: The complete trustworthiness of God's written Word, the Bible, that is wholly useful and true for Christian faith and practice.

Infinity: Without limitation and immeasurable.

Jesus Christ: The Second Person of the Holy Trinity. Jesus Christ is the Great Mediator between God and man, the King of kings and the Lord of lords, and the Savior of the world.

Joy: The inner strength, comfort and encouragement from the Holy Spirit, especially amidst the trials and tribulations of life.

Justice of God: Morally balancing the scales. God's application of equity toward inequity in the universe.

Kindness of God: God's generous patience and care, often meant to lead us to a better place.

Kingdom of God: Although closely related, the kingdom of God and the church are distinct. The kingdom of God creates the church and is brought into the world through Jesus Christ. The sovereign rule of Christ assures us that though Satan is the "god of this age" his destruction is final. Only through faith in Jesus Christ can human beings enter the Kingdom.

Logos: The Greek term for "Word." The Gospel of John teaches us that Jesus Christ is the Word that became a human being. This should not be confused with the Bible. Jesus Christ is not the Bible which is the Word of God given to humanity. Jesus Christ is the truth of God that creates and sustains all things.

Mercy of God: The goodness of God applied toward our suffering and guilt.

Nature of God: The tangible and intangible qualities and characteristics of God revealed to humanity through His Word.

New Jerusalem: The city of God where His eternal glory shines and believers abide forevermore.

Omnipotence: The all-powerful, infinite capability and energy of God.

Omnipresence: The all-present Spirit of God; at all places, equally, and simultaneously.

Omniscience: The all-knowing, perfect and complete knowledge of God — including eternity past, eternity future, and the infinite multiplicity of potential realities that could have been or may be.

Peace: An internal experience as a result of being brought into right relationship with God by the cross. Internal peace is also something the Christian may experience through the filling of the Holy Spirit.

Persecution: The systematic hostility, oppression, and mistreatment of Christ followers because of Jesus' Name.

Prayer: The act of communicating with God through thoughts, words, and even groans words cannot express but the Holy Spirit interprets. Believers have access to God in prayer through the Holy Spirit and the shed blood of Jesus Christ.

Presence of God: The particular manifestation of God: 1) in His heavenly dwelling, and 2) to the Christian experientially through the Holy Spirit.

Propitiation: The complete satisfaction of God's Holy wrath for sin through Christ's sacrifice.

Providence: The non-biblical term which comes from the Greek word "*pronoeo*" which means "to foresee," "to have regard," "to provide," and "to perceive." That is, in God's foreknowledge, God can look ahead or provide in advance.

Repentance: The act of completely turning away from one's sin through heartfelt regret and sorrow and toward God in sincere faith.

Resurrection: 1) The literal, bodily resurrection of Christ, and 2) the future bodily resurrection from the dead of all humanity. Believers in Jesus Christ will rise to eternal life with God and unbelievers will rise to judgment and eternal condemnation.

Righteousness: 1) A quality of God characterized by His faithfulness and justice, 2) a standard of moral uprightness to which human beings are held accountable, 3) morally upright or virtuous conduct, and 4) the state of being in right standing with God through faith in Jesus Christ.

Salvation: 1) The act of being brought into right standing with God through faith in Jesus Christ, 2) The process of becoming more like Jesus Christ, and 3) The final state of the believer in their glorified heavenly body.

Sanctification: The aspect of salvation whereby one becomes more and more setapart for God as they become more like Jesus Christ.

Satan: The being who opposes the purposes of God. Satan is especially associated with deceit, temptation, accusation, and testing, through which he seeks to pull Christians away from God.

Saving Faith: Complete belief and trust in the finished work of Christ on the cross for the forgiveness of one's sins and eternal life.

Sin: Humanity's broken relationship with God through disobeying His moral law. The result of individual sin is: 1) guilt, and 2) the debt of punishment.

Sinful Nature: The inherited nature passed down from Adam. It is the part of you that rebels against God and His moral law and is at war for your soul.

Self-Existence: The uncaused, eternal existence of God that had no beginning.

Self-Sufficiency: The complete and total sufficiency of God within Himself. God is not dependent upon anything or anyone outside of Himself.

Soul: The Greek term for soul is "*psyche*" and refers to the unseen, inner life of a person.

Sovereignty: God's exercise of His supremacy in the universe.

Special Revelation: The particular revelation of God and His plan of salvation through the Person of Jesus Christ and the inspired, written Word of God.

Supernatural: A manifestation or event associated with a force outside of the laws of nature or the scientific method.

Supremacy: The absolute and universal rule of God over the universe. God is supreme over the works of His Hands and His governing over the wills of men.

The Church: The local and universal body of believers, both past, present, and future. The Greek term for church, "*ekklesia,*" means "an assembly" and is derived from two Greek words, "*ek*" meaning "out of" and "*kaleo*" meaning "to call." The church are the ones called out of the world.

The Cross: The roman invention designed for brutal torture and shameful punishment. The cross was God chosen method to satisfy His Holy wrath for sin.

The Enemy: The unseen, spiritual forces of evil who oppose God and are antagonistic toward Christians, namely Satan and the demons.

The Fall: The departure of creation and human beings from the patterns and standards originally set by God. The Fall is a direct consequence of Adam's sin and impacts every aspect of the person, including the mind, the will, the emotions, and even the conscience.

The Father: The First Person of the Holy Trinity. The Father is the source of divine love toward humanity, the basis of encouragement through Scripture, the answerer ofprayer, and the sender of the Son and the Spirit.

Throne: The Greek term for throne is "*thronos*" and refers literally and figuratively to the seat of authority.

Transcendence: The categorically set apart nature of God that: 1) exists separate from creation, and 2) is not subject to the limitations of creation.

Unapproachable Light: The inaccessibility of sinful human beings to see God in the natural state, for God is too Holy to look upon.

Union with Christ: The identification of the believer in relationship to Jesus Christ, particularly His death and resurrection for the forgiveness of sins and eternal life. Union with Christ brings immediate removal of all condemnation for sin.

Unveil: To uncover, reveal or disclose.

Veil: To cover, conceal, or hide.

Veracity: The quality of truthfulness, correctness, and accuracy.

Worship: Complete reverence and exaltation for who God is and what God has done through head, heart, hands, and speech.

Wrath: The Holy fury and anger of God toward sin. The wrath of God satisfied through the cross is a direct result of God's love and justice in action against sin.

Notes

A 30-Day Meditation

1. Romans 12:2a (NLT).
2. Philippians 1:9 (NIV).
3. A.W. Tozer, *The Knowledge of the Holy*. Harper Collins, 1961.

Preface: Thinking Rightly of God & His Holy Attributes

1. Millard J. Erickson, *Christian Theology* — 2nd Ed (Grand Rapids, Michigan: Baker Books, 1983-1998), p. 316. The entire section on Greatness and Goodness is found on pp. 289-326.
2. Genesis 3:4-5 (NASB).
3. Isaiah 14:12-16.
4. Romans 1:23 (ERV).
5. John 8:44b-c (NLT).
6. 2 Corinthians 11:14 (NIV).

Day 1: The Self-Existence of God

1. A.W. Pink, *The Attributes of God*, Baker Books, 1975.
2. Genesis 1:3.
3. Genesis 1:26.
4. Job 36:26a (NIV).
5. 2 Corinthians 5:15 (HCSB).
6. Daniel 4:33-34.

Day 2: The Self-Sufficiency of God

1. Exodus 3:14.
2. Colossians 1:17 (NLT).
3. John 4:24 (ESV).
4. Matthew 16:24 (ERV).
5. John 8:12 (TPT).
6. Acts 3:19 (TPT).

Day 3: The Incomprehensibility of God

1. Hebrews 10:20 (TPT).
2. 1 Corinthians 3:16 (GNT).
3. John 19:30a (NASB).
4. Ephesians 3:12 (TPT).

Day 4: The Infinity of God

1. 2 Thessalonians 1:8-9 (NCV).
2. John 3:16 (NIV).
3. Romans 8:11 (GW).
4. Philippians 3:12-14.
5. John 17:3 (MSG).

Day 5: The Eternity of God

1. Psalm 90:2 (NIV).
2. Ecclesiastes 3:11b (GW).
3. Genesis 3:22 (GNT).
4. Genesis 3:24.
5. Romans 5:8 (TPT).
6. Ephesians 1:14.
7. 2 Corinthians 5:4d-5 (NLV).

Day 6: The Holiness of God

1. Revelation 4:8b (NKJV).
2. Isaiah 6:5 (NASB).
3. Job 42:5-6 (NIV).
4. James 1:17a (TPT).
5. Deuteronomy 4:24 (CSB).
6. Christina Delgado, editor.
7. Hebrews 10:10 (NET Bible).
8. John 15:19b (NIV).
9. Martin Lloyd-Jones, *Lloyd-Jones on the Christian Life: Doctrine and Life as Fuel and Fire.* Crossway, 2018.
10. James 3:4-5.
11. Proverbs 8:13a (NIV).
12. Psalm 27:8 (NIV).
13. Brother Lawrence, *The Practice of the Presence of God with Spiritual Maxims*, Baker Book Publishing House, 1958.

Day 7: The Oneness of God

1. Ephesians 5:23 (MSG).
2. Philippians 2:2b (CEV).

Day 8: The Holy Trinity

1. Colossians 1:16.
2. Colossians 2:9 (NLT).
3. 1 Timothy 2:5 (ESV).
4. Ecclesiastes 1:8b (CEV).

Day 9: The Impeccability of God

1. Psalm 68:5-6a (TPT).
2. James 1:13b (HCSB).
3. Philip Yancey, "*The Jesus I Never Knew*," Zondervan, 1993.
4. Luke 22:42 (NLT).
5. Ephesians 1:7 (TPT).
6. John 16:13.
7. 2 Samuel 22:31a-b.
8. Deuteronomy 8:3 (NIV).
9. Proverbs 3:5-6 (ERV).
10. Hebrews 10:14 (NET Bible).

Day 10: The Transcendence of God

1. A.W. Tozer, *The Knowledge of the Holy.*
2. Proverbs 9:10 (GNT).
3. Isaiah 46:10 (NLT)
4. John 11:25.
5. Hebrews 12:28 (NET Bible).

Day 11: The Immanence of God

1. Acts 17:27-28a (MSG).
2. John 16:7.
3. John 14:20 (TPT).
4. Saint Athanasius of Alexandria, *On the Incarnation of the Word of God.*
5. 2 Corinthians 3:18b-c (ERV).
6. Ezekiel 36:26a.
7. 2 Corinthians 5:17.
8. Hebrews 4:15 (CEV).

9. Zephaniah 3:17 (GNT).
10. Luke 12:7b (MSG).
11. Acts 17:28a (NIV).

Day 12: The Omnipresence of God

1. Hebrews 11:3 (TPT).
2. Psalm 90:5-6.
3. 2 Corinthians 4:18.
4. 1 Peter 1:7.
5. Hebrews 4:13.
6. Romans 2:16.
7. Proverbs 5:21 (NLT).
8. John 3:18 (NLT).
9. Matthew 28:20.

Day 13: The Immutability of God

1. Malachi 3:6 (KJV).
2. Isaiah 43:13a (NLT).
3. Hebrews 13:8 (CEV).
4. Psalm 62:2 (ISV).
5. Philippians 2:12.

Day 14: The Omniscience of God

1. Colossians 3:3 (TPT).
2. Saint Augustine of Hippo, *The Confessions of Saint Augustine.*
3. Isaiah 43:1b-3a (MSG).
4. 2 Corinthians 5:7 (ESV).
5. Philippians 4:6-7.
6. Psalm 139:17 (TPT).

Day 15: The Providence of God

1. James 1:13b (NASB).
2. Genesis 50:20 (NIV).
3. Matthew 26:13 (MSG).
4. Romans 8:28a (TPT).
5. 1 Corinthians 1:25 (GNT).
6. 1 Corinthians 13:12a (NLT).

Day 16: The Omnipotence of God

1. Institute of Physics.
2. Genesis 1:16b (CEV).
3. Romans 1:20 (MSG).
4. 2 Peter 1:3 (CSB).
5. Matthew 16:24.
6. James 1:5.
7. Colossians 1:11 (TPT).
8. Ephesians 1:19-20 (NLT).

Day 17: The Supremacy of God

1. Colossians 1:15.
2. Colossians 1:16.
3. Isaiah 66:1a (NIV).
4. Isaiah 29:13a-b.
5. Psalm 50:21 (CSB).
6. James 4:15 (CEB).
7. Galatians 5:1a (GNT).
8. John 10:28-29.
9. John 16:33b (MSG).
10. Colossians 2:15.
11. Romans 8:37.
12. Ephesians 2:6.

Day 18: The Sovereignty of God

1. Proverbs 16:9 (TPT).
2. Isaiah 55:8-9 (NLT).

Day 19: The Veracity of God

1. Robert L. Deffenbaugh, *The Truth of God*, Bible.org (2004).
2. John 12:49.
3. Psalm 119:105.
4. Luke 4:4.
5. 2 Timothy 3:16.
6. 1 Peter 1:25.
7. Psalm 19:1 (GW).
8. 2 Corinthians 4:6 (GNT).
9. John 1:1 (NIV).
10. John 1:14 (NIV).
11. Revelation 21:1-4.
12. Matthew 10:16b.
13. Hebrews 13:5b (CSB).
14. Romans 10:17.

Day 20: The Wrath of God

1. Dr. Larry J. Waters: "*The Warfare of Suffering*," DTS Chapel, September 27, 2017.
2. 1 John 4:10 (NLT).
3. Exodus 12:13.
4. 1 Peter 1:19 (ERV).

Day 21: The Mystery of God

1. Deuteronomy 29:29.
2. John 1:29.
3. Revelation 5:5.
4. 1 Corinthians 15:51-52 (GNT).
5. 1 Corinthians 15:13-14 (TPT).
6. William Lane Craig, "*The Son Rises*," Wipf and Stock Publishers, 2000. Italics original.
7. John 20:29 (CEV).
8. Romans 6:5.

Day 22: The Goodness of God

1. Matthew 5:45b-c (CEV).
2. 2 Corinthians 2:15b-16a (TLB).
3. Jeremiah 17:7-8 (MSG).
4. Galatians 5:22-23 (TPT).

Day 23: The Kindness of God

1. Romans 2:4d (TPT).
2. Acts 3:19.
3. Jeremiah 29:11.
4. Proverbs 31:25 (CSB).
5. Galatians 5:22.
6. Matthew 6:3.
7. Matthew 6:2.
8. Romans 2:4 (NLT).
9. Revelation 3:20.

Day 24: The Grace of God

1. Psalm 51:5.
2. Jeremiah 17:9 (GW).
3. Romans 3:23.
4. Romans 6:23.
5. Colossians 2:14b-c (TPT).
6. Isaiah 64:6 (MSG).
7. Proverbs 16:2 (GNT).
8. Hebrews 12:15 (TPT).
9. Matthew 18:32b-33a (TPT).

Day 25: The Mercy of God

1. Hebrews 4:16.
2. 2 Corinthians 1:3.
3. Psalm 145:9.
4. Titus 3:5.
5. Isaiah 53:4 (ESV).
6. 1 Peter 2:24 (MSG).
7. C.S. Lewis, *The Problem of Pain*, Harper Collins, 1940.
8. Romans 8:1.
9. Colossians 1:22.
10. Matthew 23:37b-c (GW).
11. Psalm 119:132 (NIV).
12. Luke 6:36 (NIV).
13. Matthew 6:21 (TPT).
14. Proverbs 27:19 (NIV).
15. Psalm 89:14.

Day 26: The Love of God

1. 1 John 4:8b (NIV).
2. Isaiah 54:10 (GWT).
3. Saint Augustine of Hippo (uncited).
4. Psalm 23:6 (TPT).
5. Psalm 30:11 (TPT).
6. Luke 19:10.
7. Matthew 4:19.
8. Matthew 5:44-45a (ERV).
9. Matthew 7:16.
10. Colossians 3:14 (TPT).

Day 27: The Faithfulness of God

1. 2 Timothy 2:13 (HCSB).
2. Hebrews 11:1 (ISV).
3. Jude 24.
4. 1 Thessalonians 5:23b-24 (GW).
5. Ephesians 2:8-9.
6. Ephesians 1:11-14.
7. Genesis 4:7b-c.
8. V. Raymond Edman, *The Disciplines of Life*, Van Kampen Press, 1948.
9. Psalm 139:13.
10. Deuteronomy 7:9.

Day 28: The Justice of God

1. Proverbs 16:2 (NIV).
2. Hebrews 4:12.
3. Psalm 19:12 (CSB).
4. Isaiah 64:6.

5. Romans 3:10b.
6. Psalm 51:4.
7. Romans 3:4b (NIV).
8. Philippians 2:10-11.
9. Matthew 5:38.
10. Matthew 5:41.
11. Matthew 5:44;
12. Micah 6:8 (NIV).
13. Isaiah 58:6.
14. Revelation 21:4; Isaiah 25:8.

Day 29: The Joy of God

1. Nehemiah 8:10.
2. Romans 8:28.
3. 1 Peter 1:7.
4. James 1:2-4 (NLT).
5. Acts 16:31-34.
6. Isaiah 53:10-11.
7. Hebrews 12:2b.
8. Psalm 16:8 (NIV).
9. Ephesians 2:6 (CEV).
10. Romans 8:38-39.
11. Colossians 3:1.

Day 30: The Peace of God

1. John 14:27 (CEV).
2. Ephesians 2:5.
3. Isaiah 9:6.
4. Colossians 1:20b.
5. Romans 5:1 (ERV).

6. Colossians 1:6b (TPT).
7. Psalm 23:1-2 (TPT).
8. 1 Samuel 13:14.
9. Psalm 51:7.
10. Philippians 4:6-7.
11. Ephesians 6:12 (CEV).
12. 1 John 4:4.
13. Ephesians 6:10-18.
14. 1 Peter 5:7.
15. Philippians 4:4-7.
16. Matthew 5:9 (NIV).
17. Ephesians 5:1-2.
18. Colossians 3:13 (CEV).
19. Matthew 5:24.

Meditating on God's Holy Attributes

1. Genesis 1:28.
2. Matthew 6:13.
3. Psalm 46:10a (NIV).
4. John 3:3.
5. John 12:25 (MSG).
6. Romans 12:2a (NLT).
7. 1 Corinthians 15:33 (NIV).
8. Psalm 1:2 (MSG).
9. John 16:13a (NIV).
10. 2 Timothy 2:16 (NIV).
11. Mother Teresa of Calcutta (uncited).
12. Matthew 6:3 (NIV).
13. Psalm 146:2 (CEB).
14. Ephesians 6:12 (ERV).

English Versions

ASV *American Standard Version*

CEV *Contemporary English Version*
New York: American Bible Society (1995)

CEB *Common English Bible*
Nashville, TN: Christian Resources Development Corporation (2011)

CSB *Christian Standard Bible*
Nashville, TN: Holman Bible Publishers (2017)

ERV *Easy-to-Read Version*
Crete, IL: Bible League International (2006)

ESV *English Standard Version*
Wheaton, IL: Good News Publishers (2001)

ESVUK *English Standard Version Anglicized*
Wheaton, IL: Crossway Bibles (2001)

GNT *Good News Translation*
Philadelphia, PA: American Bible Society (1992)

GW *God's Word Translation*
Grand Rapids, MI: Baker Publishing Group (1995)

HCSB *Holman Christian Standard Bible*
Nashville, TN: Holman Bible Publishers (2009)

ISV	*International Standard Version* La Mirada, CA: Davidson Press (1995)
KJV	*King James Version*
MSG	*The Message* Colorado Springs: Navpress (1993)
MEV	*Modern English Version* Lake Mary, FL: Charisma House (2014)
NASB	*New American Standard Bible* Anaheim, CA: Foundation Press (1973)
NCV	*New Century Version* Nashville, TN: Thomas Nelson (2005)
NET Bible	*New English Translation* Richardson, TX: Biblical Studies Press (1996)
NIV	*New International Version* Colorado Springs: Biblica, Inc. (1978, 1984)
NKJV	*New King James Version* Nashville, TN: Harper Collins (1982)
NLT	*New Living Translation* Wheaton, IL: Tyndale House Publishers (1996)

TLB *The Living Bible*
Carol Stream, IL: Tyndale House Publication (1971)

TPT *The Passion Translation*
Savage, MN: Broad Street Publishing Group (2017)

72850888R00128

Made in the USA
Columbia, SC
05 September 2019